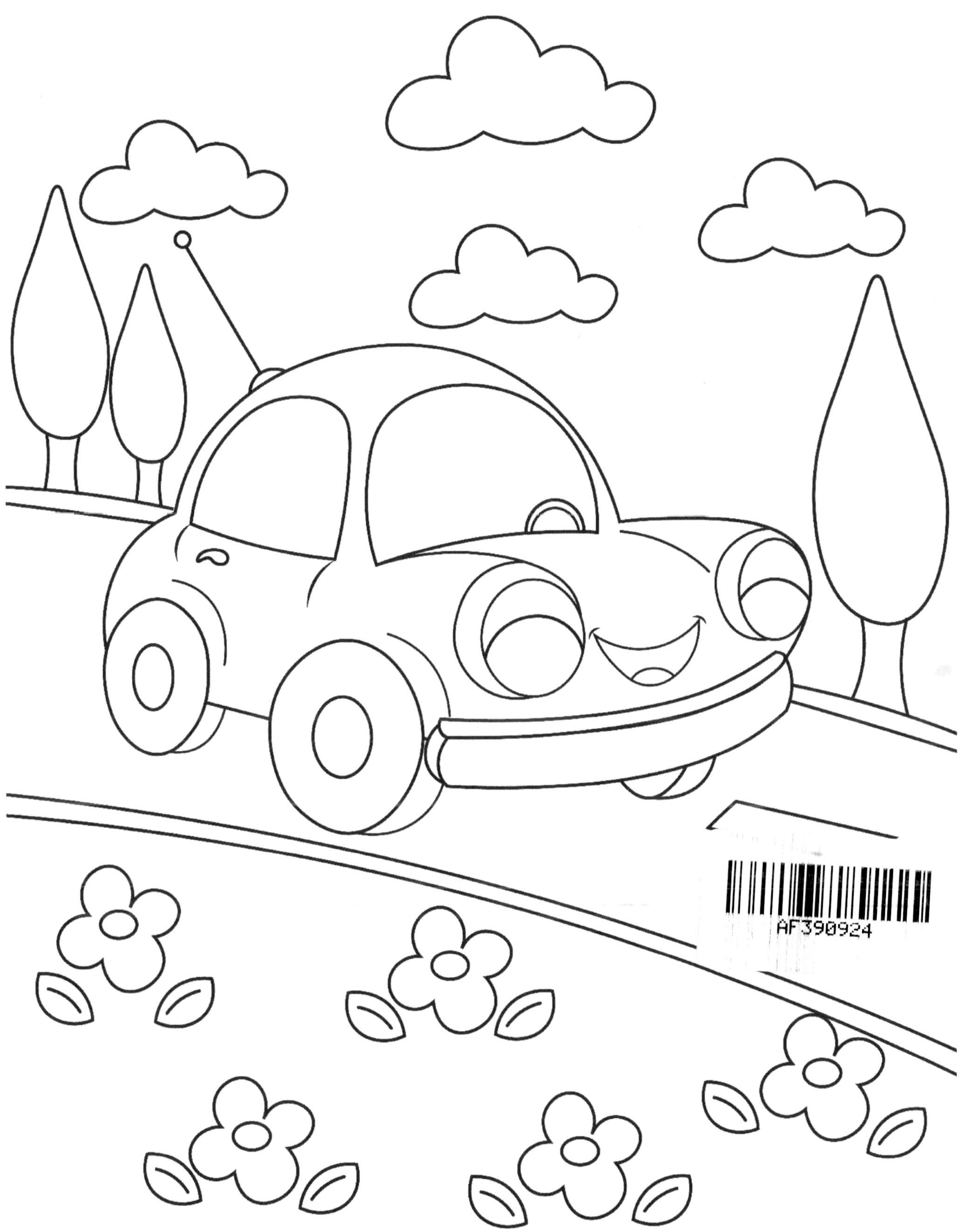
AF390924

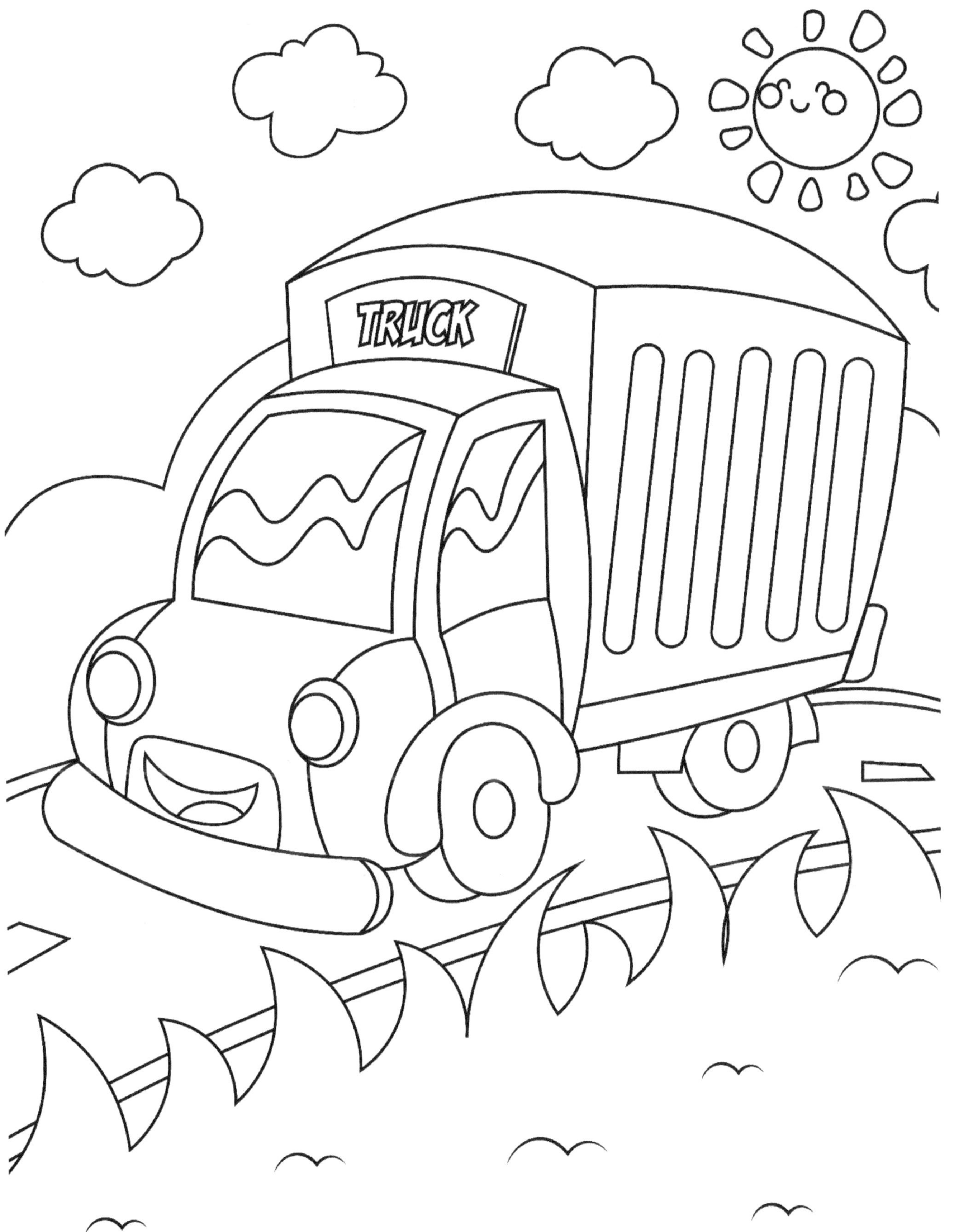
TRUCK

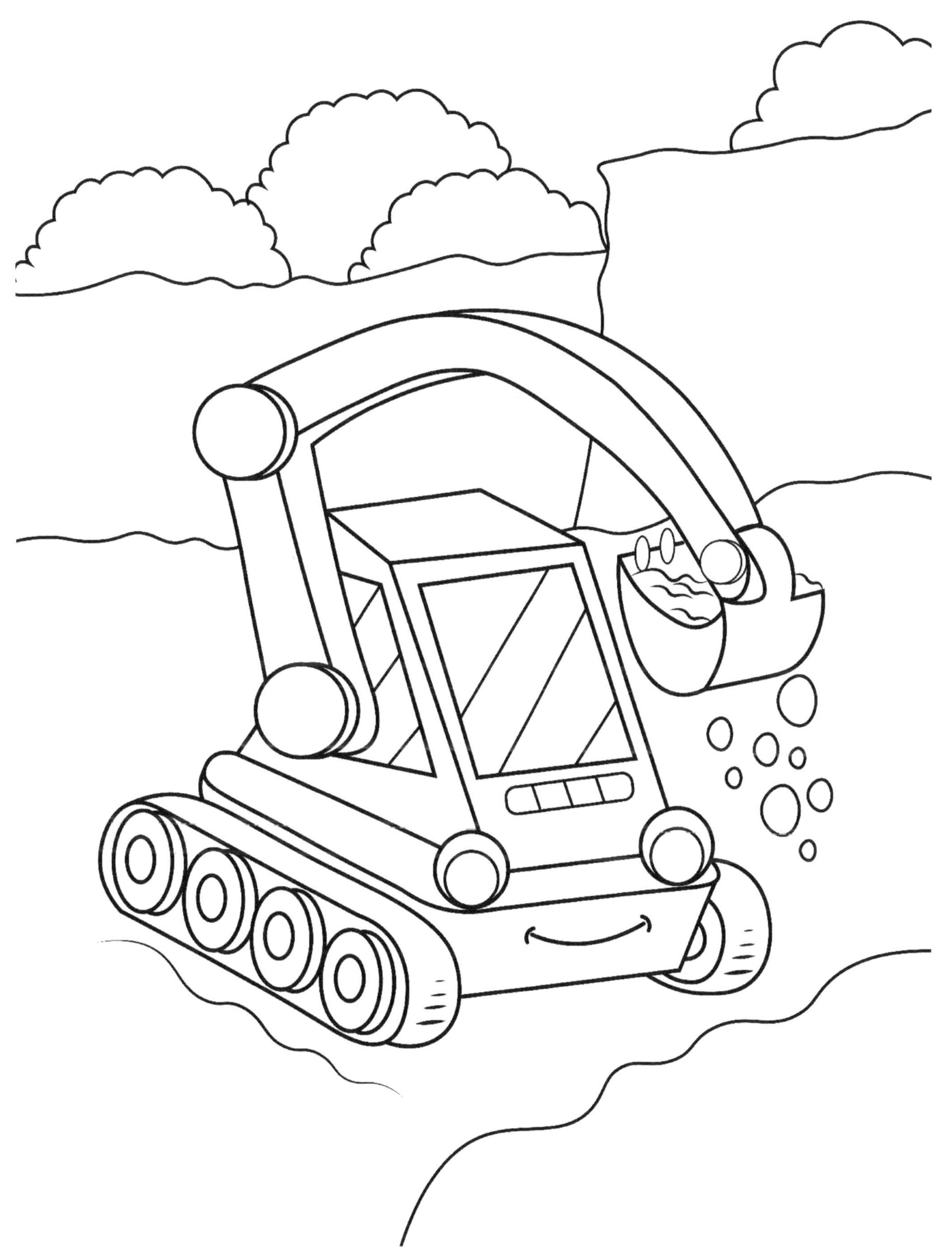

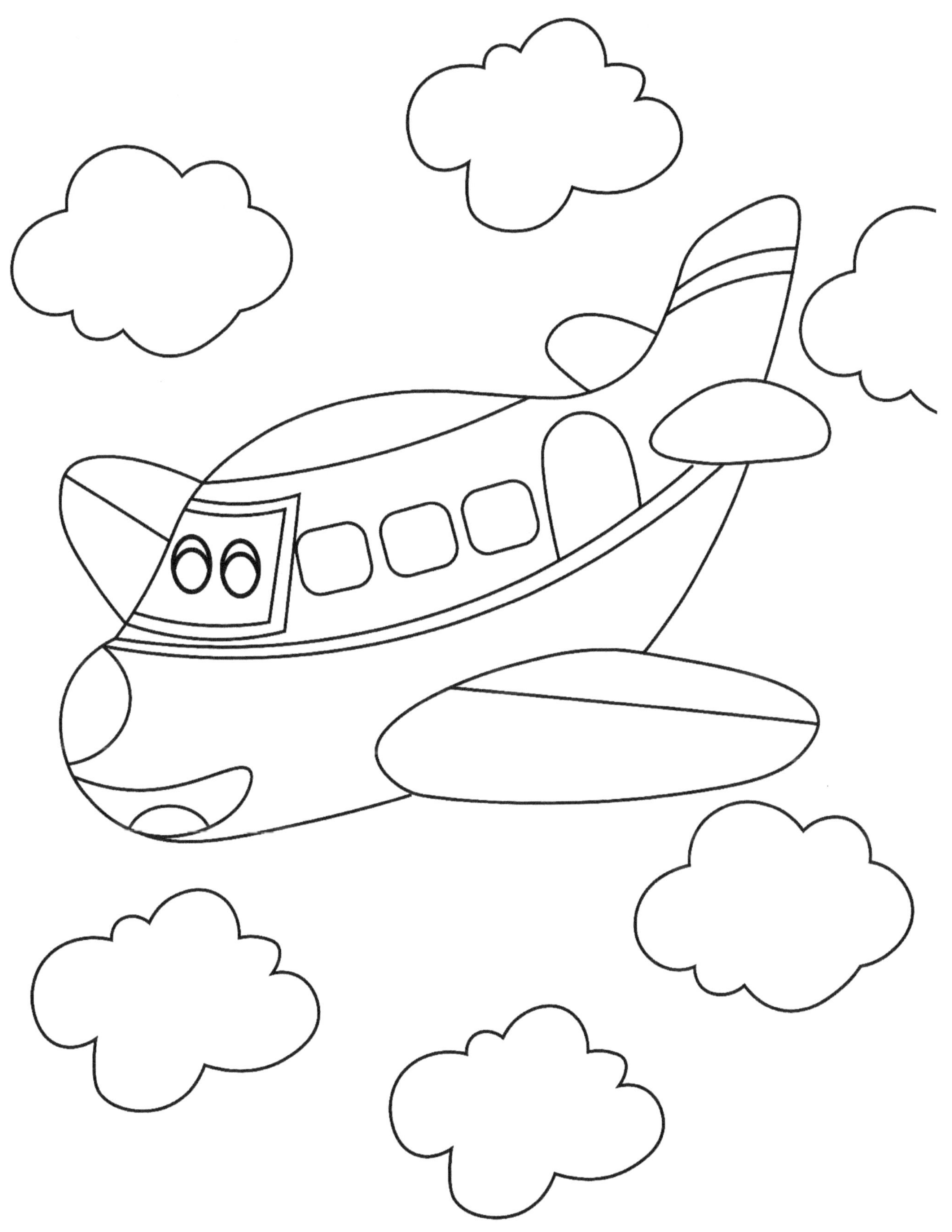

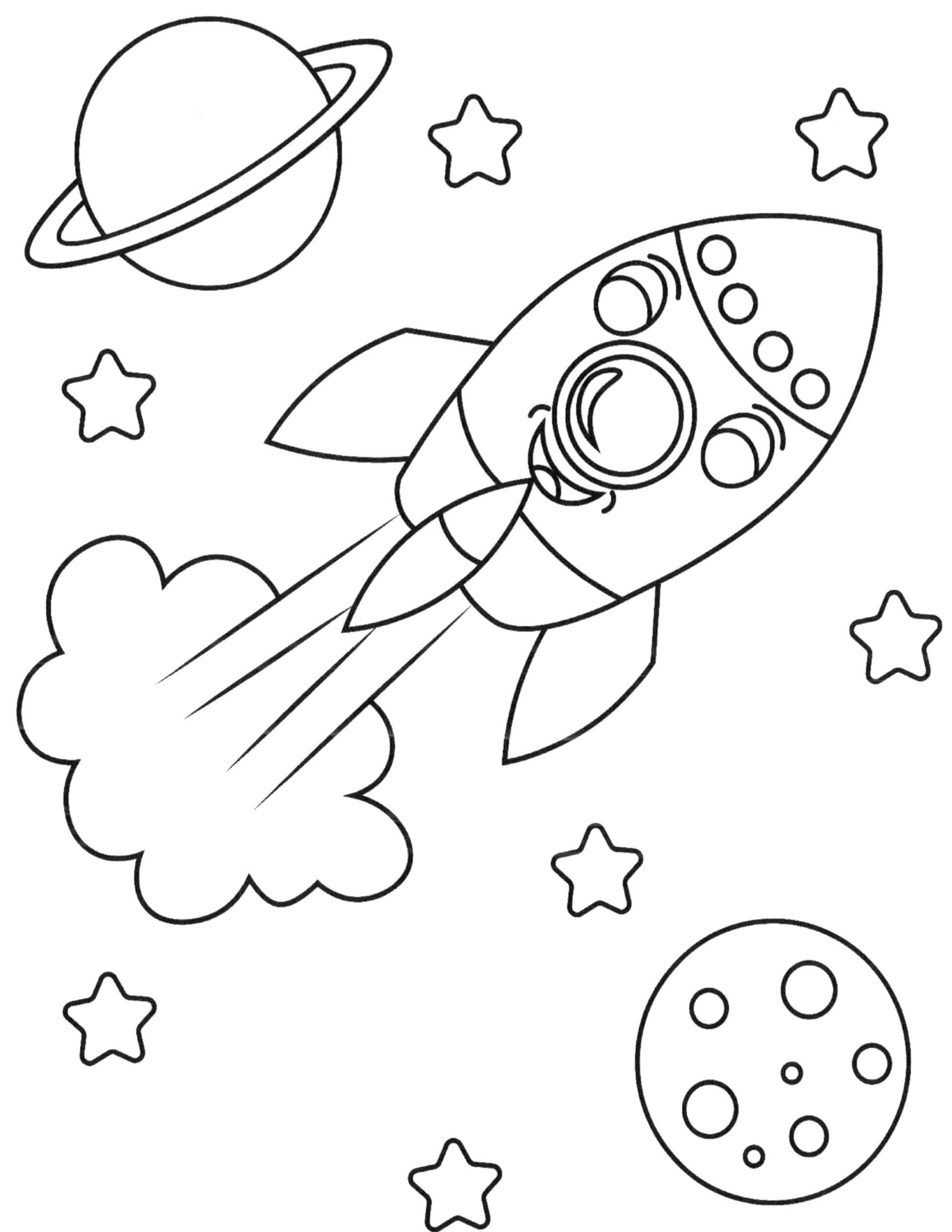

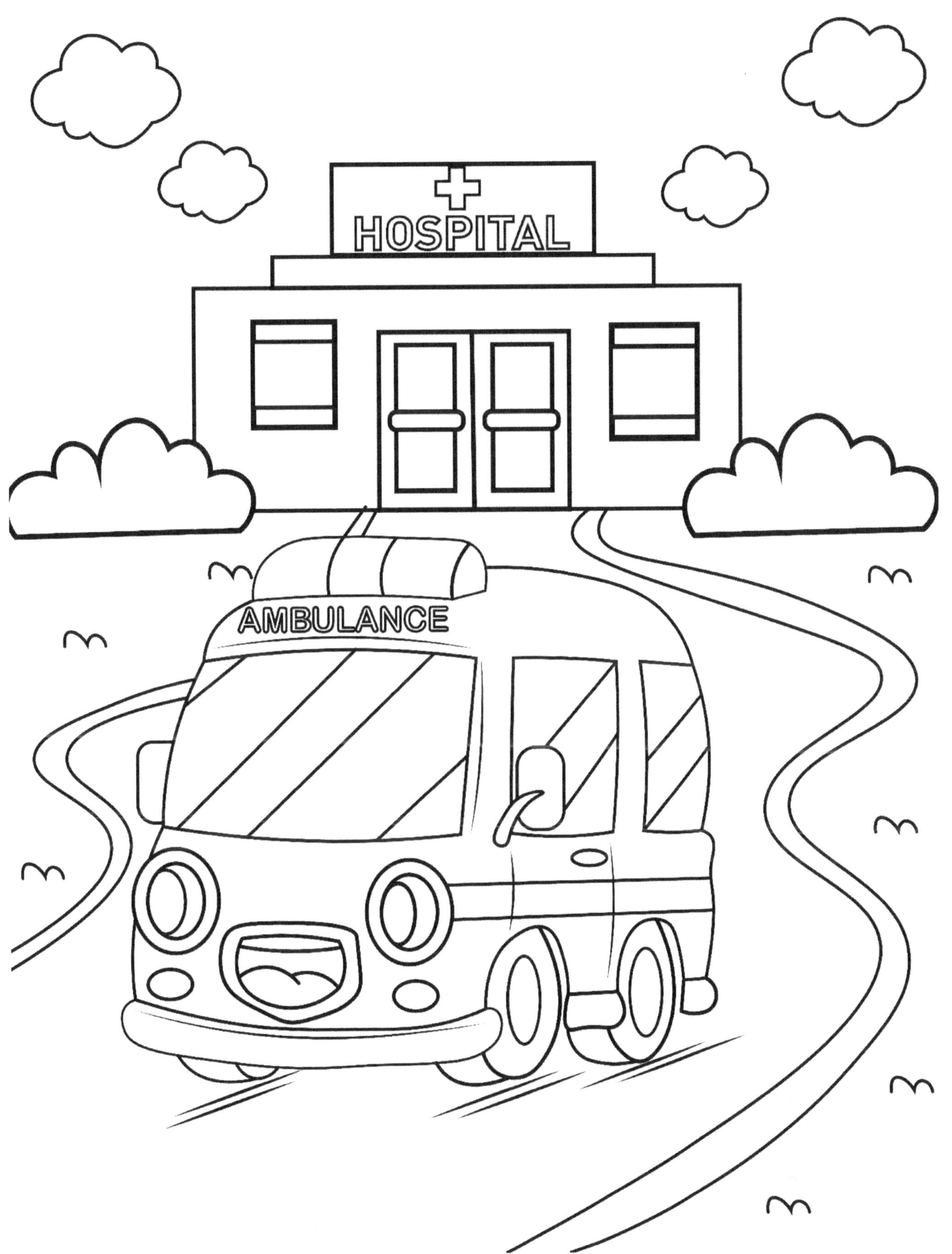

HOSPITAL
AMBULANCE

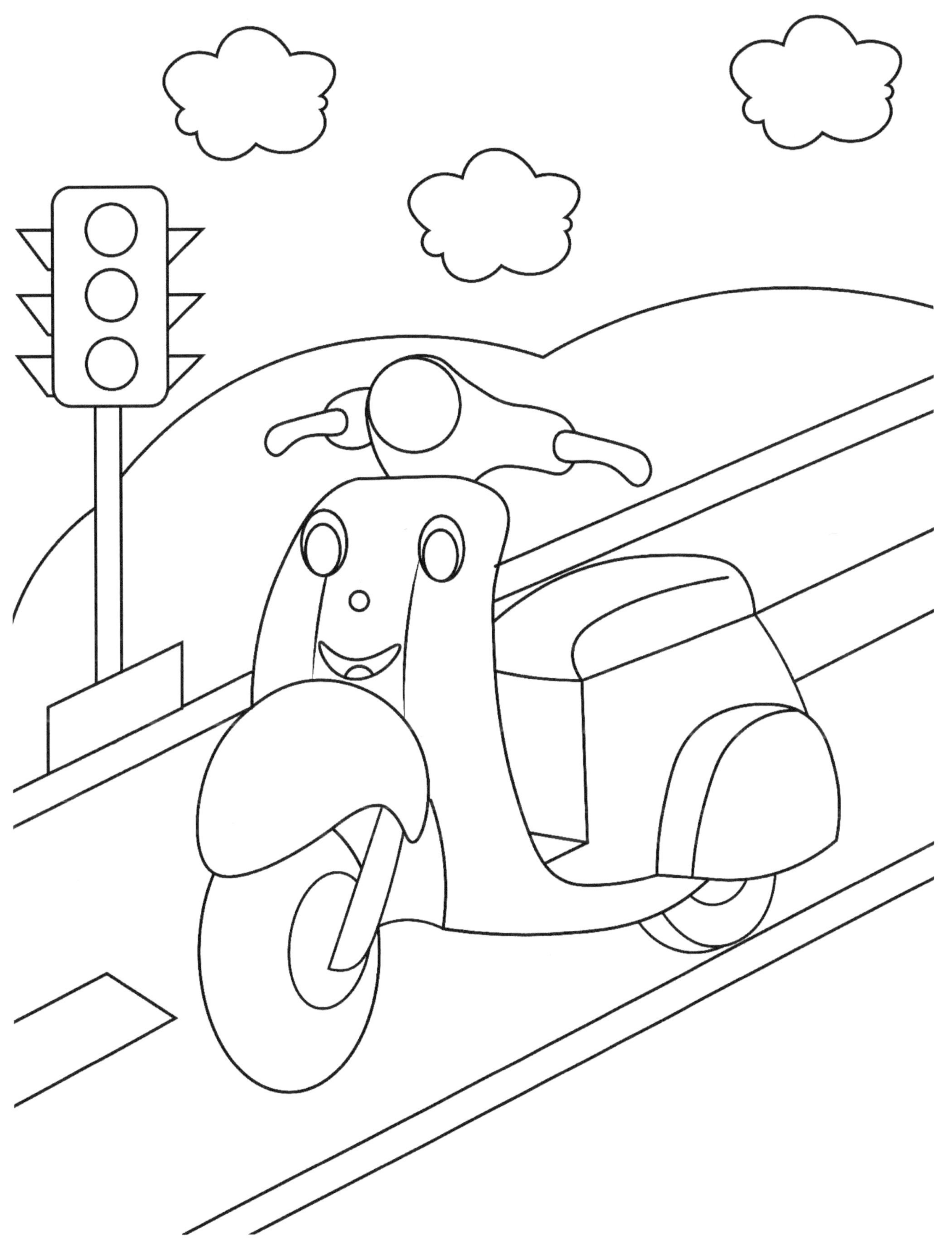

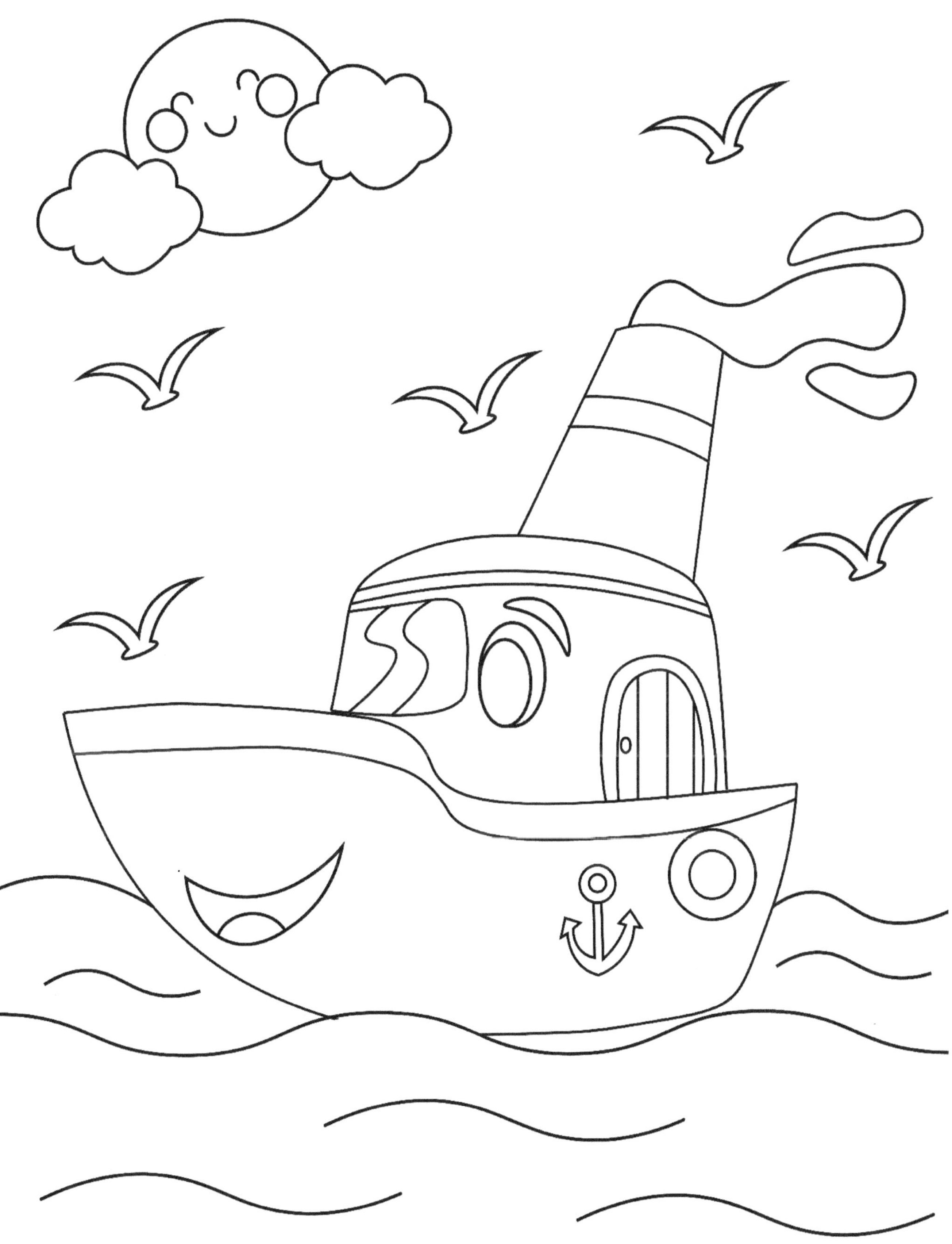

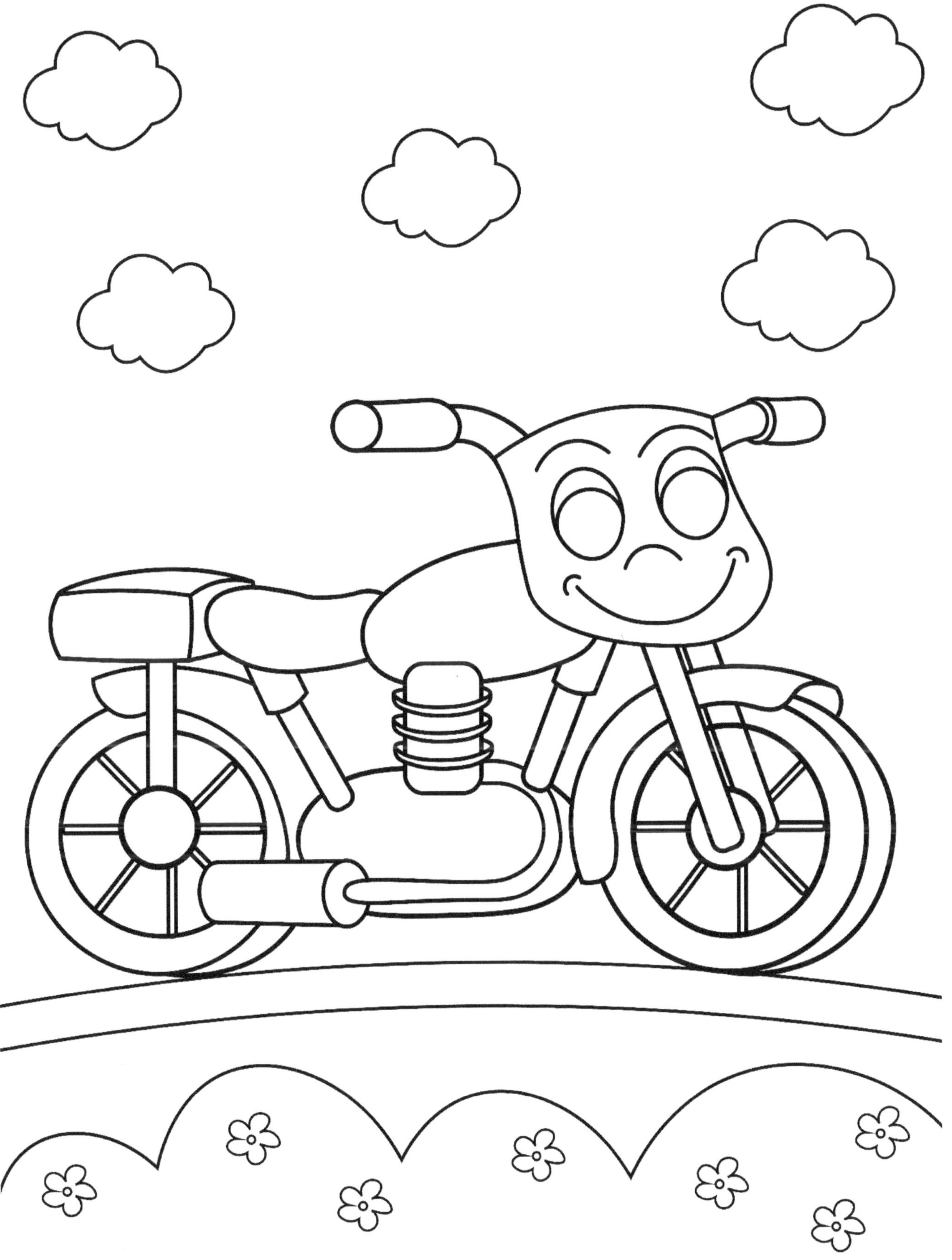

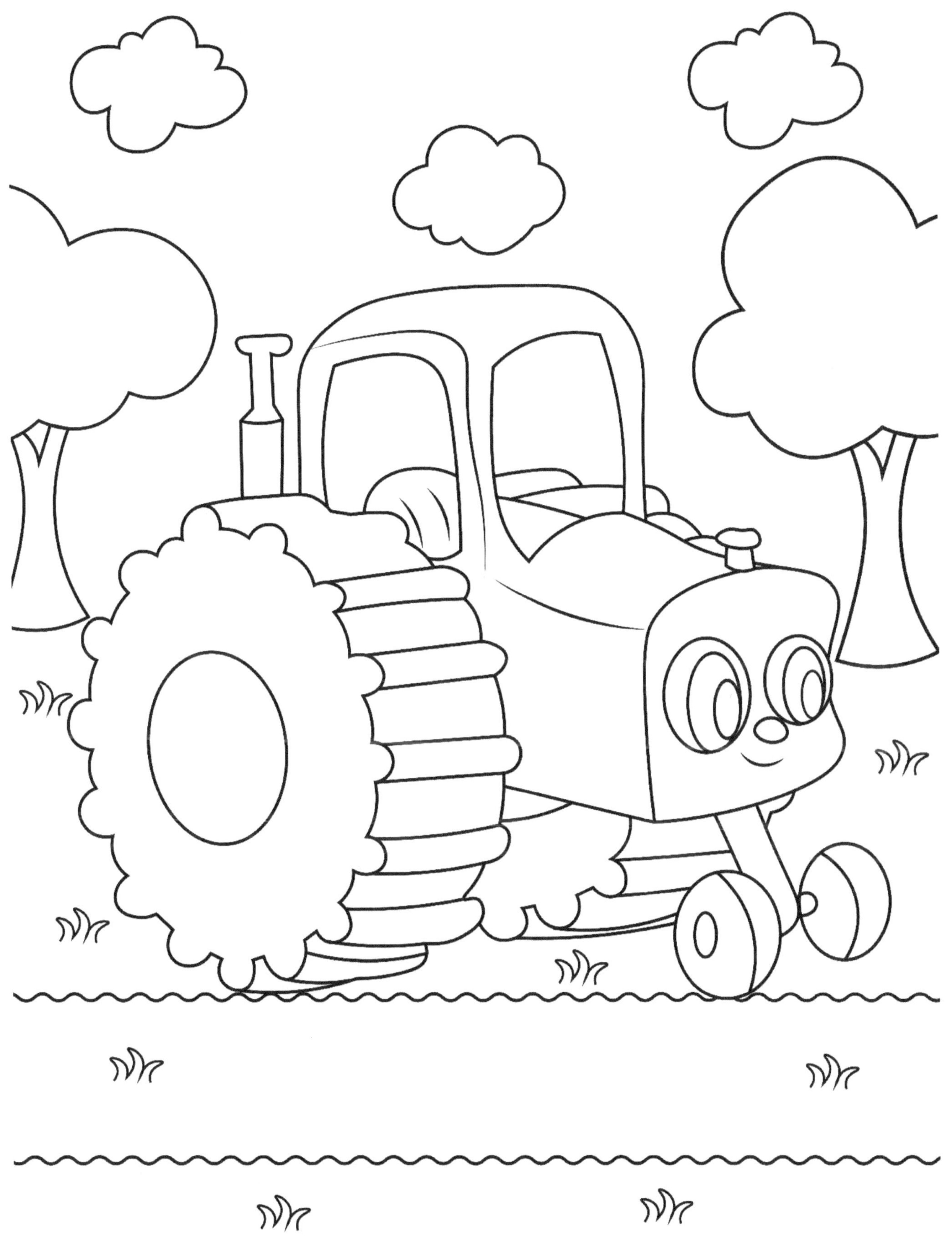

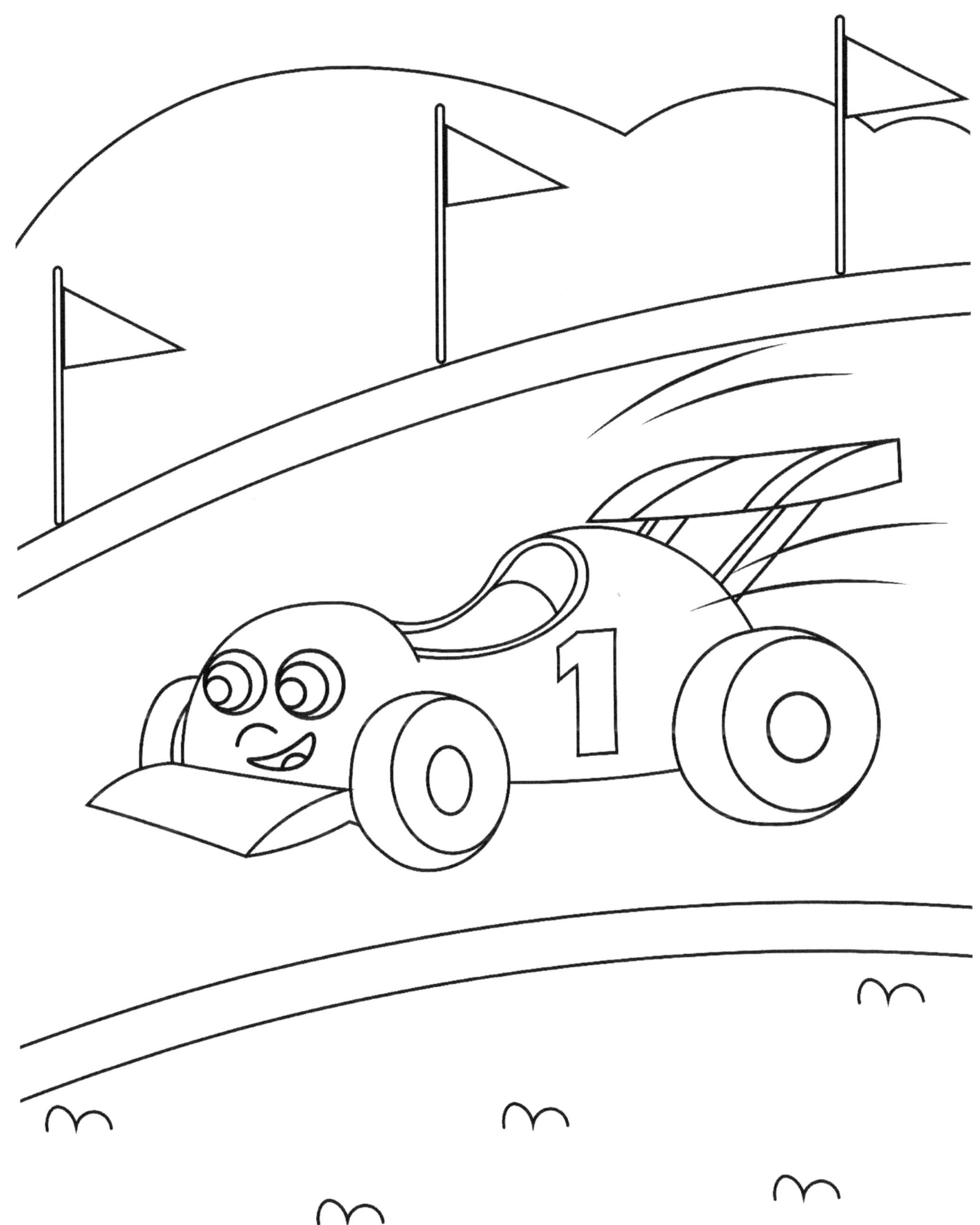

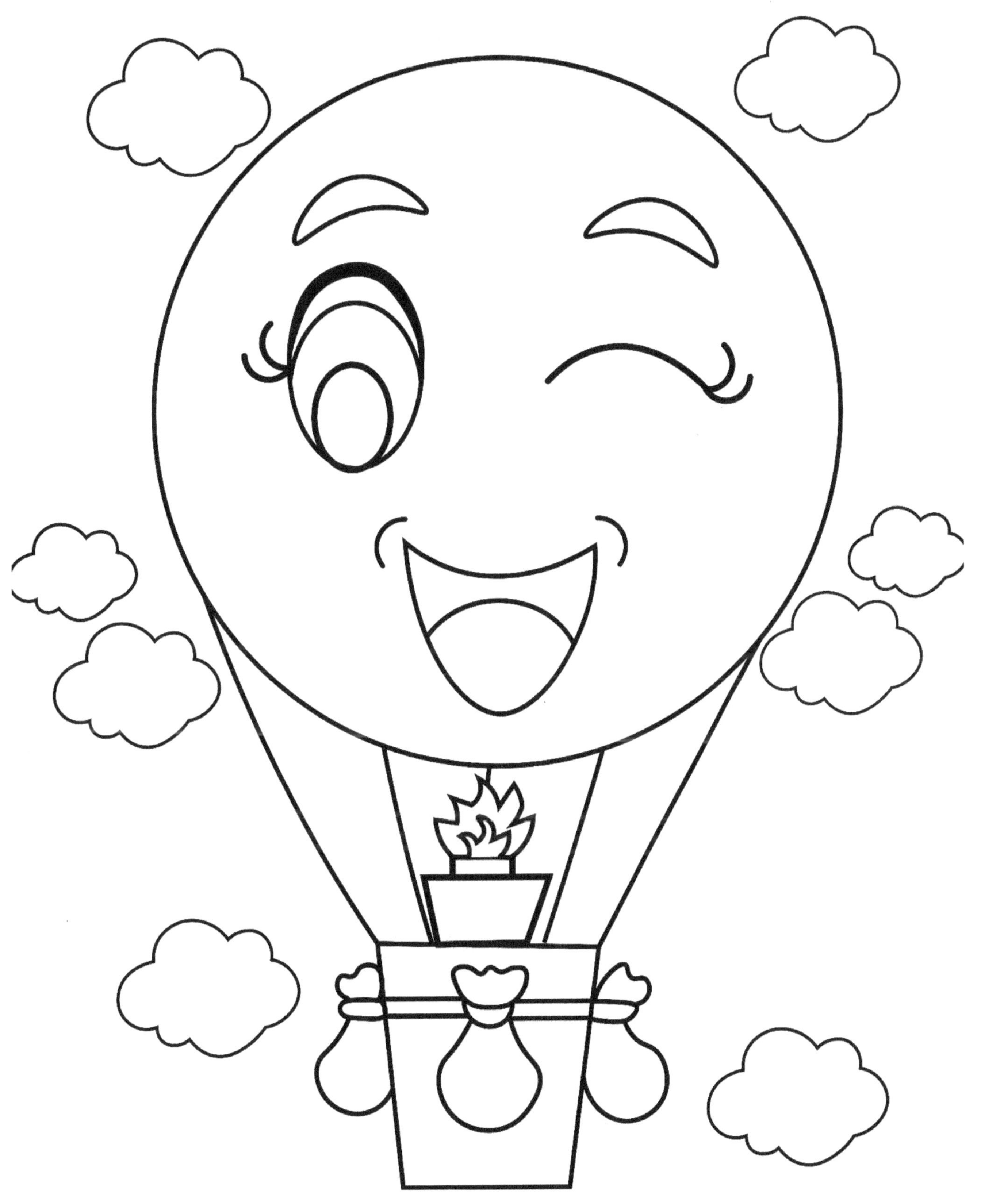

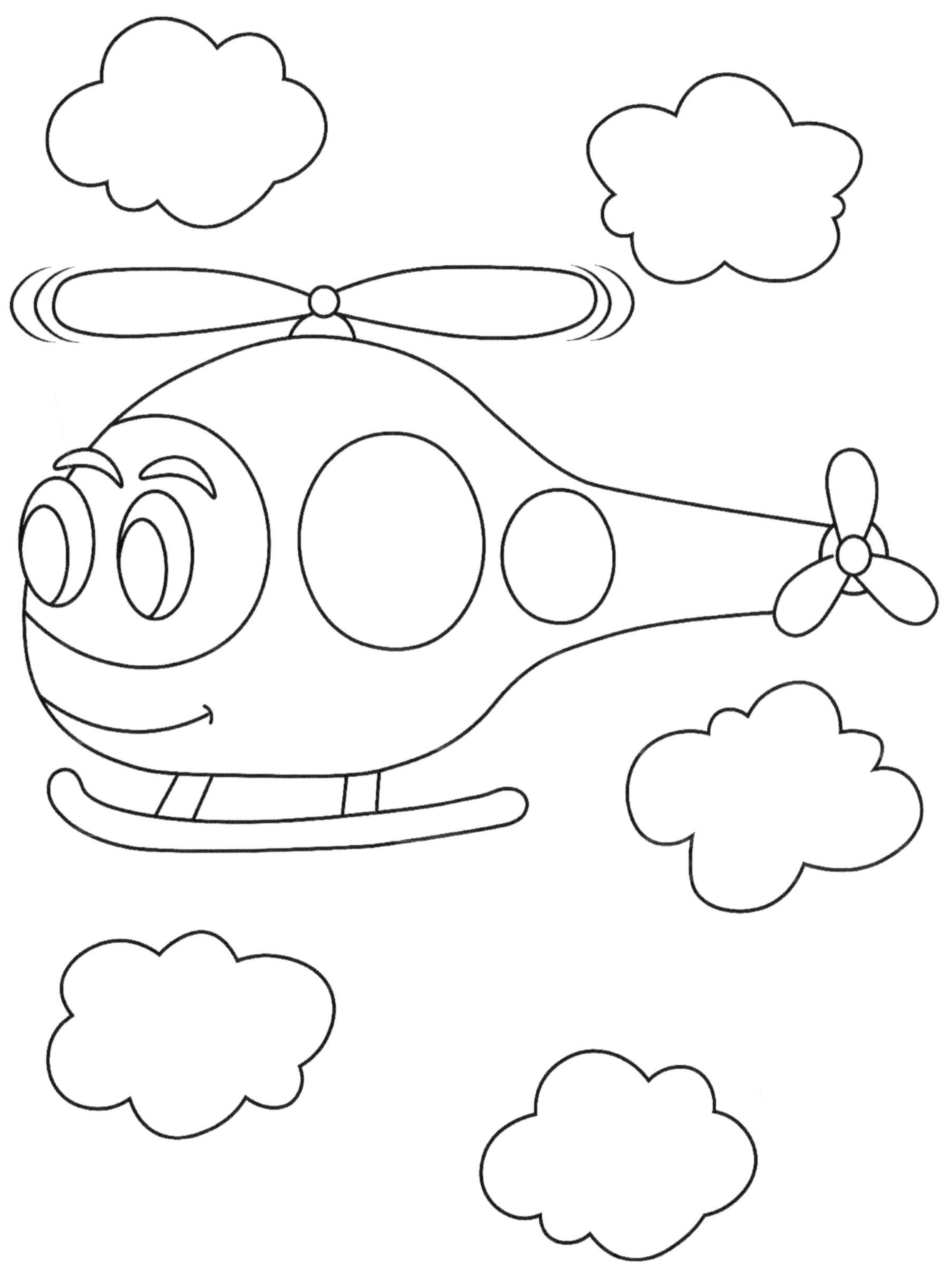

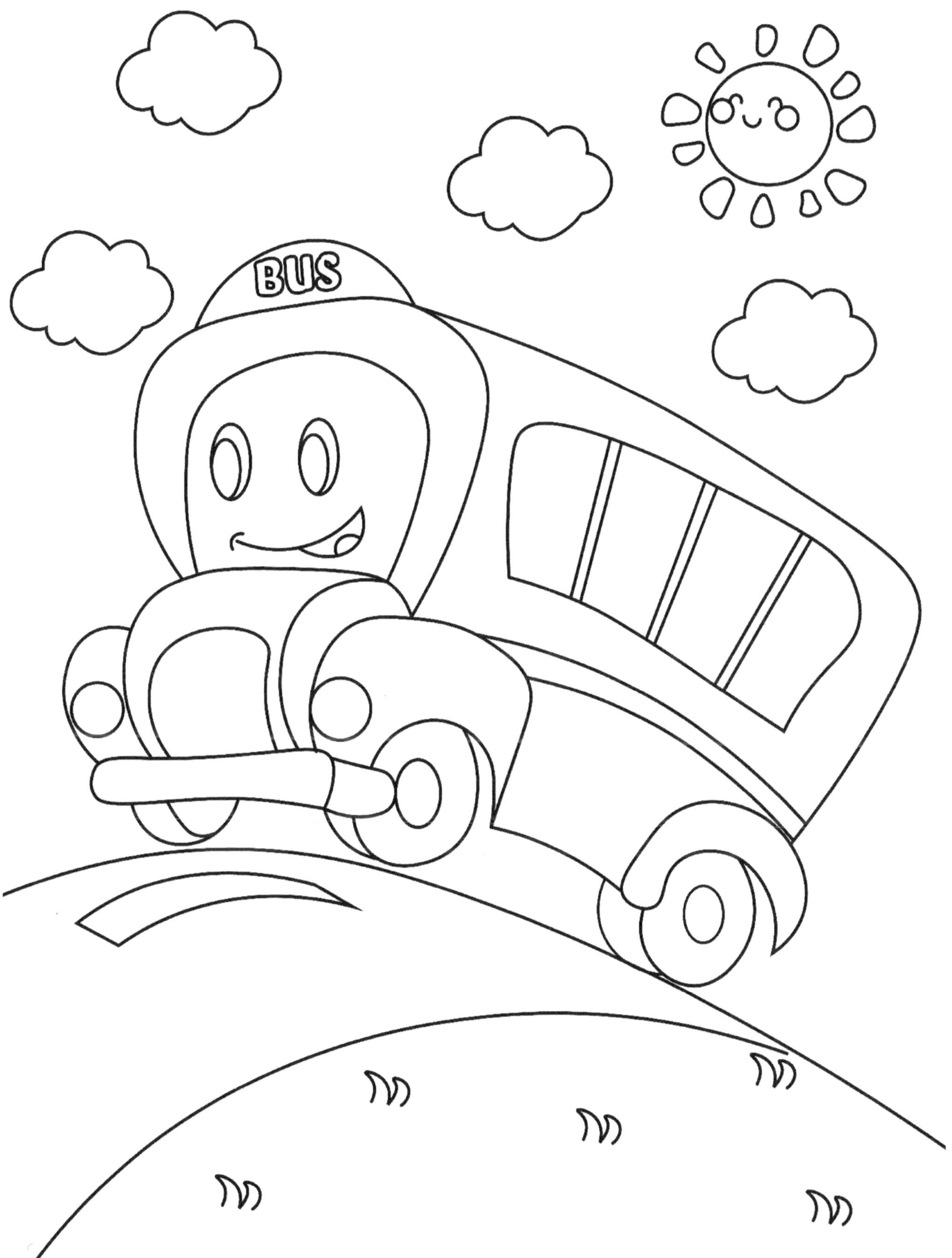
BUS

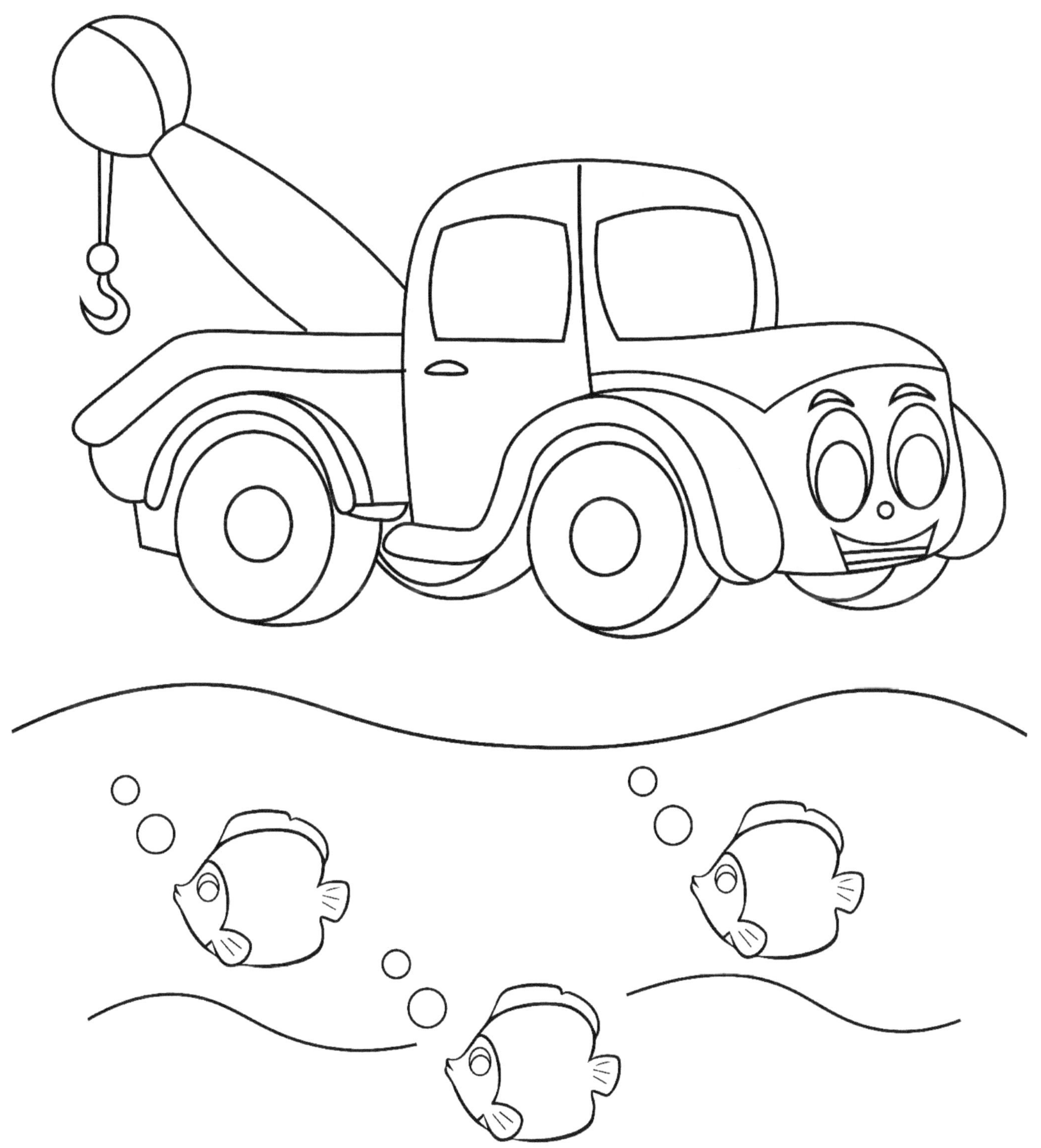

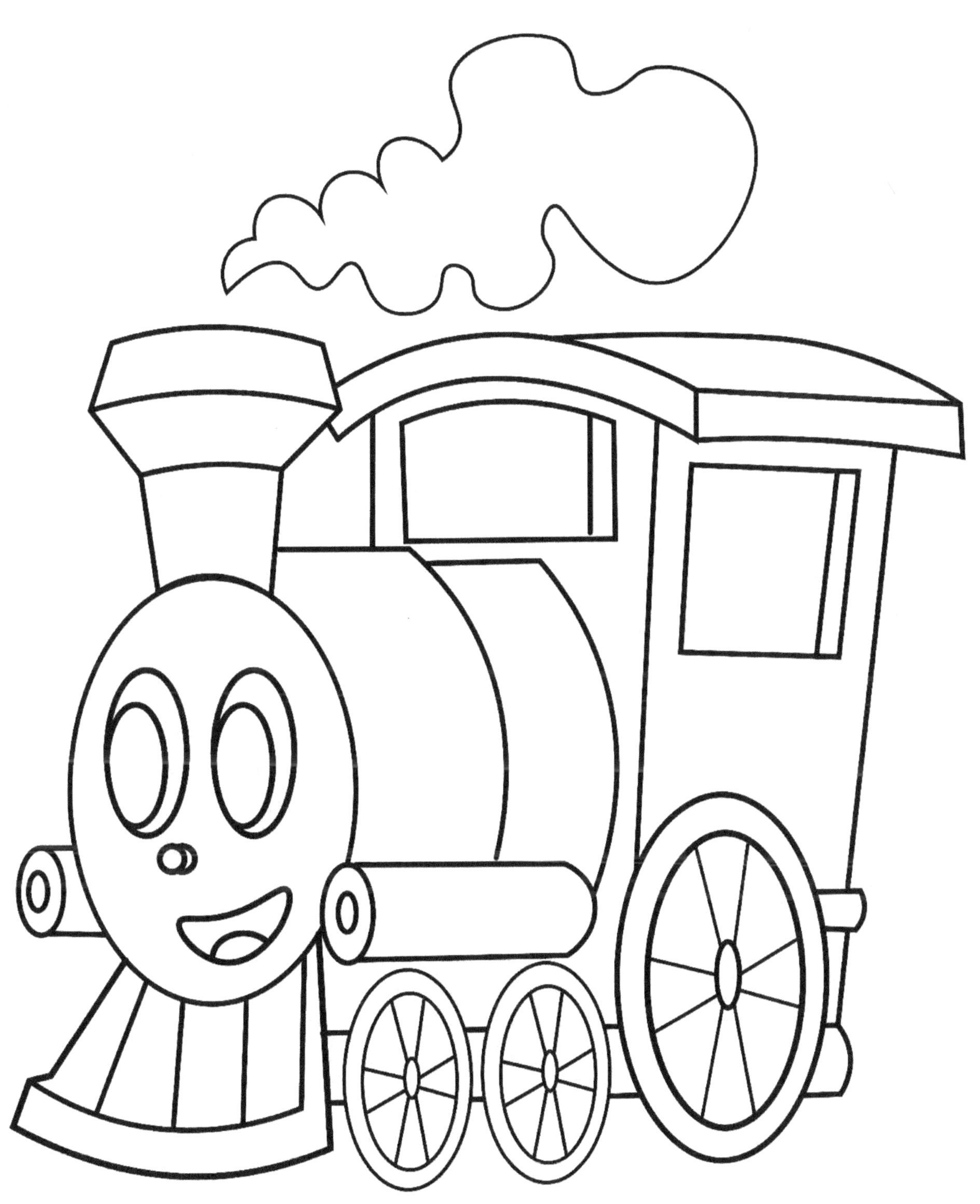

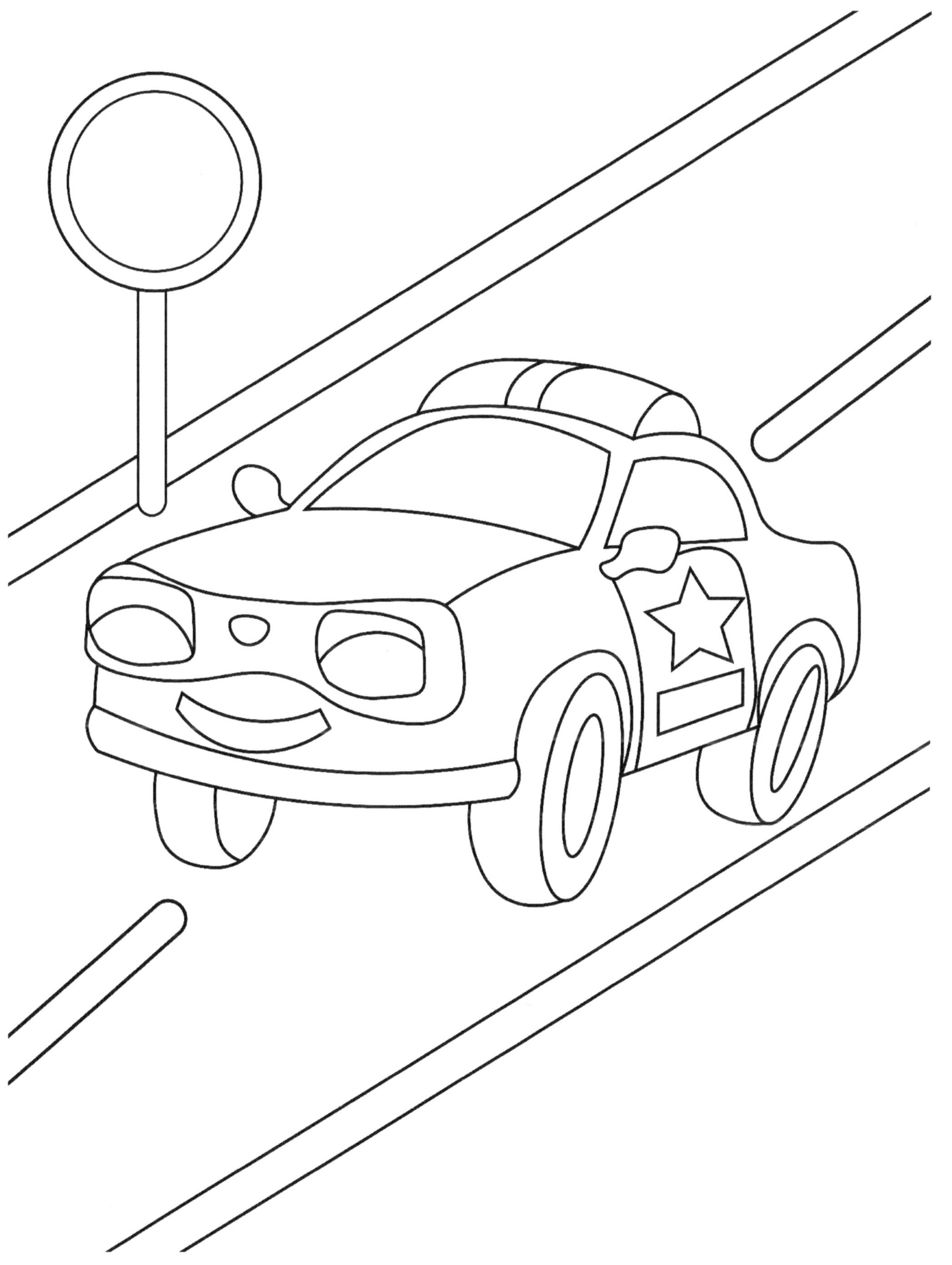

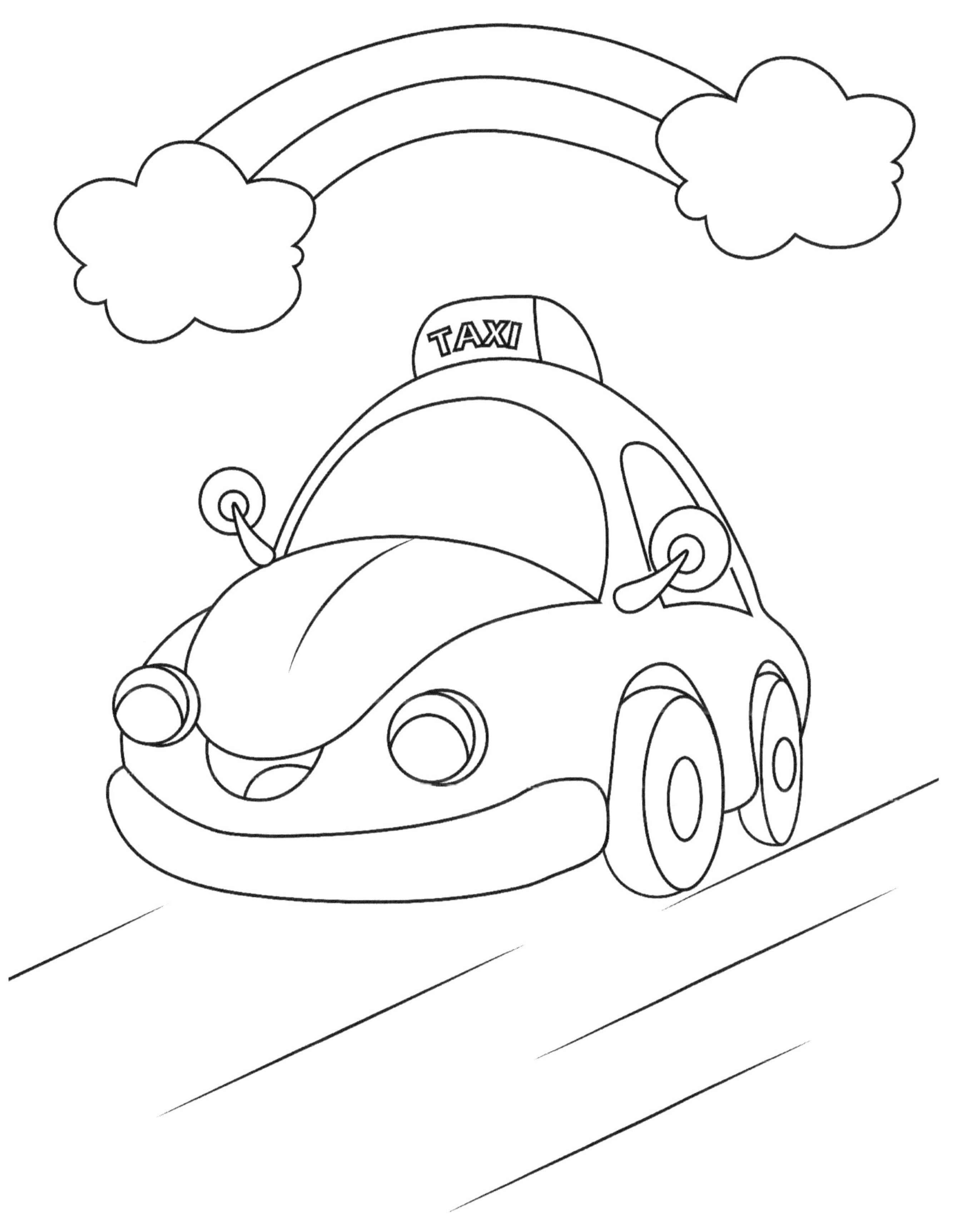

TAXI

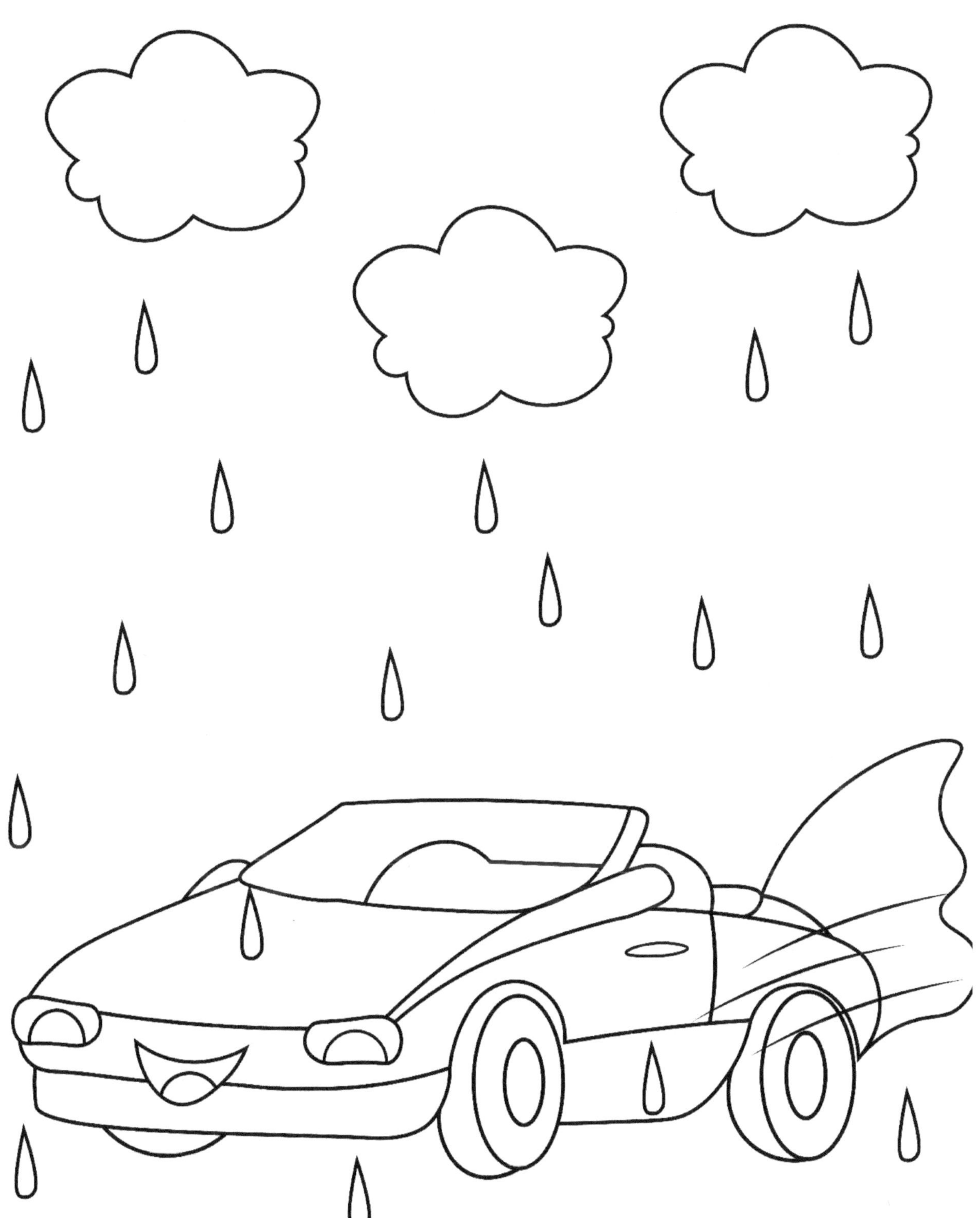

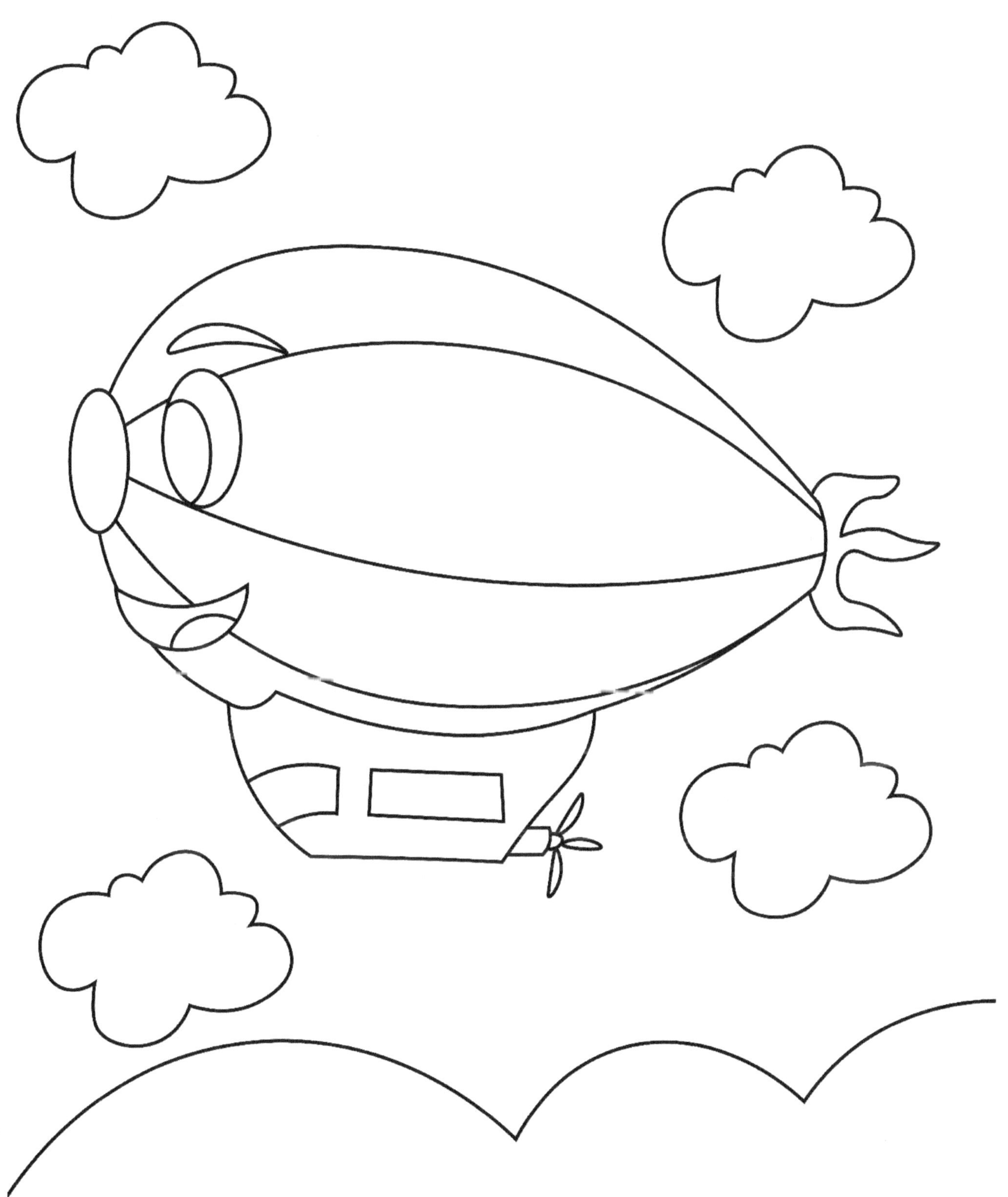

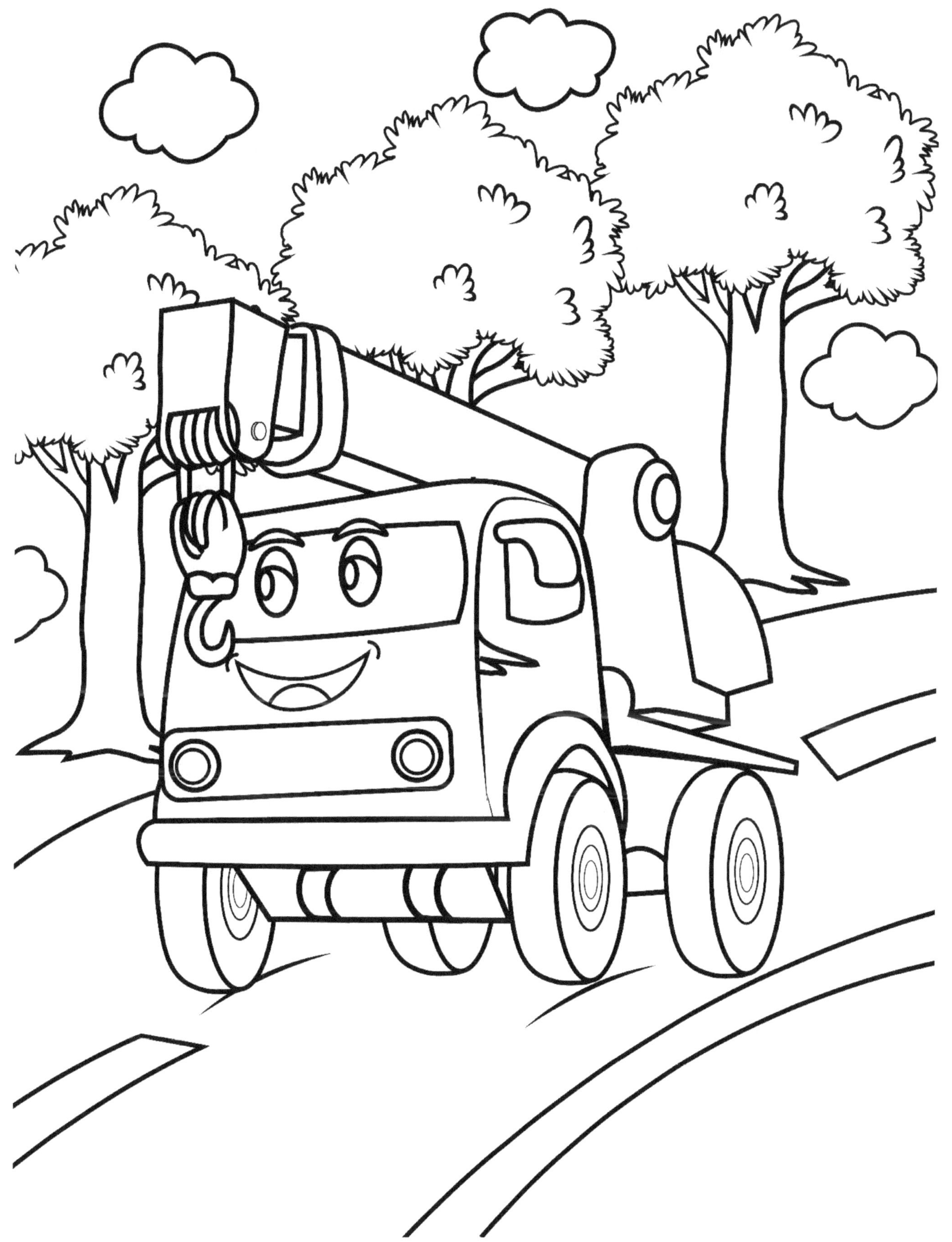

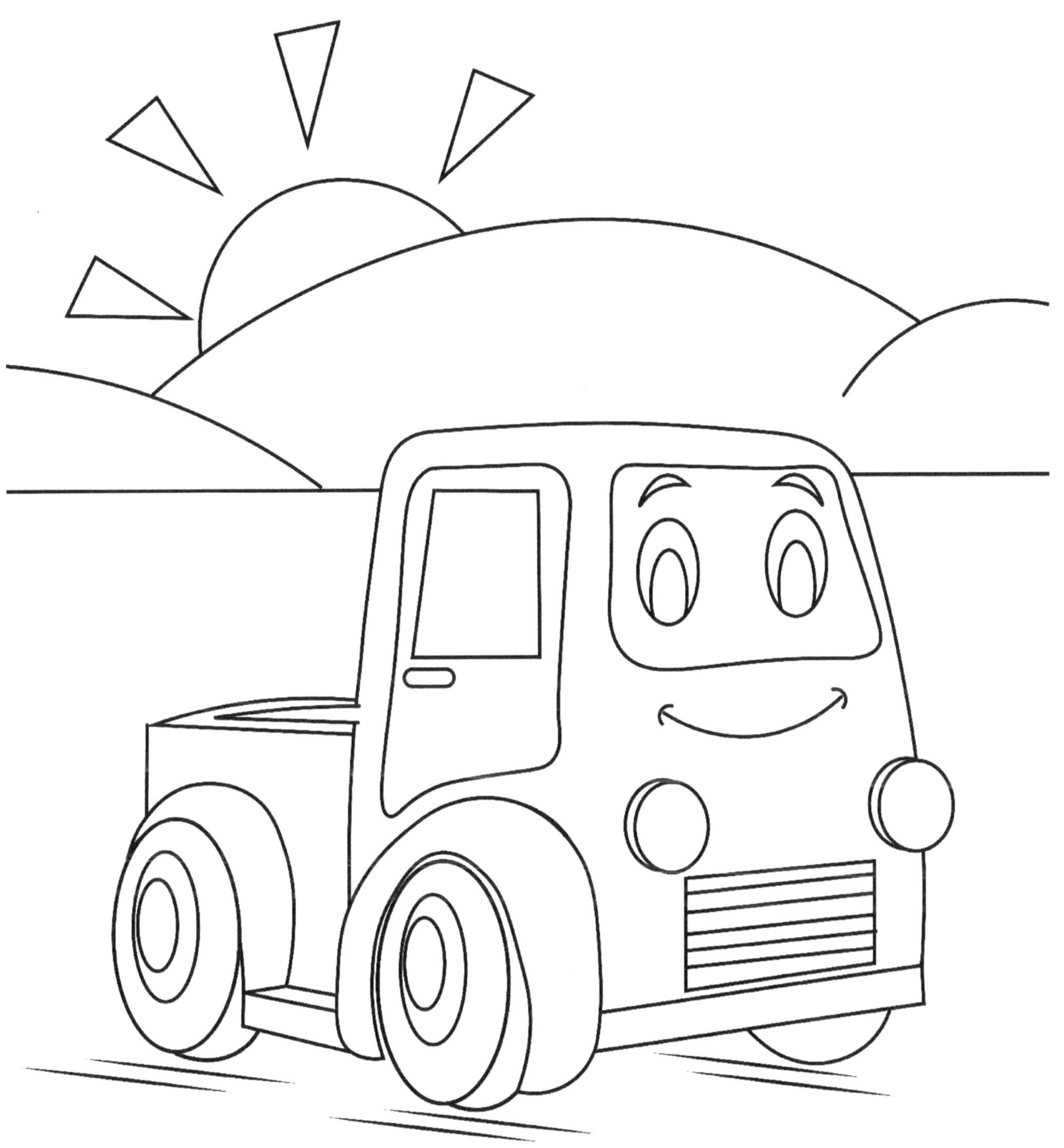

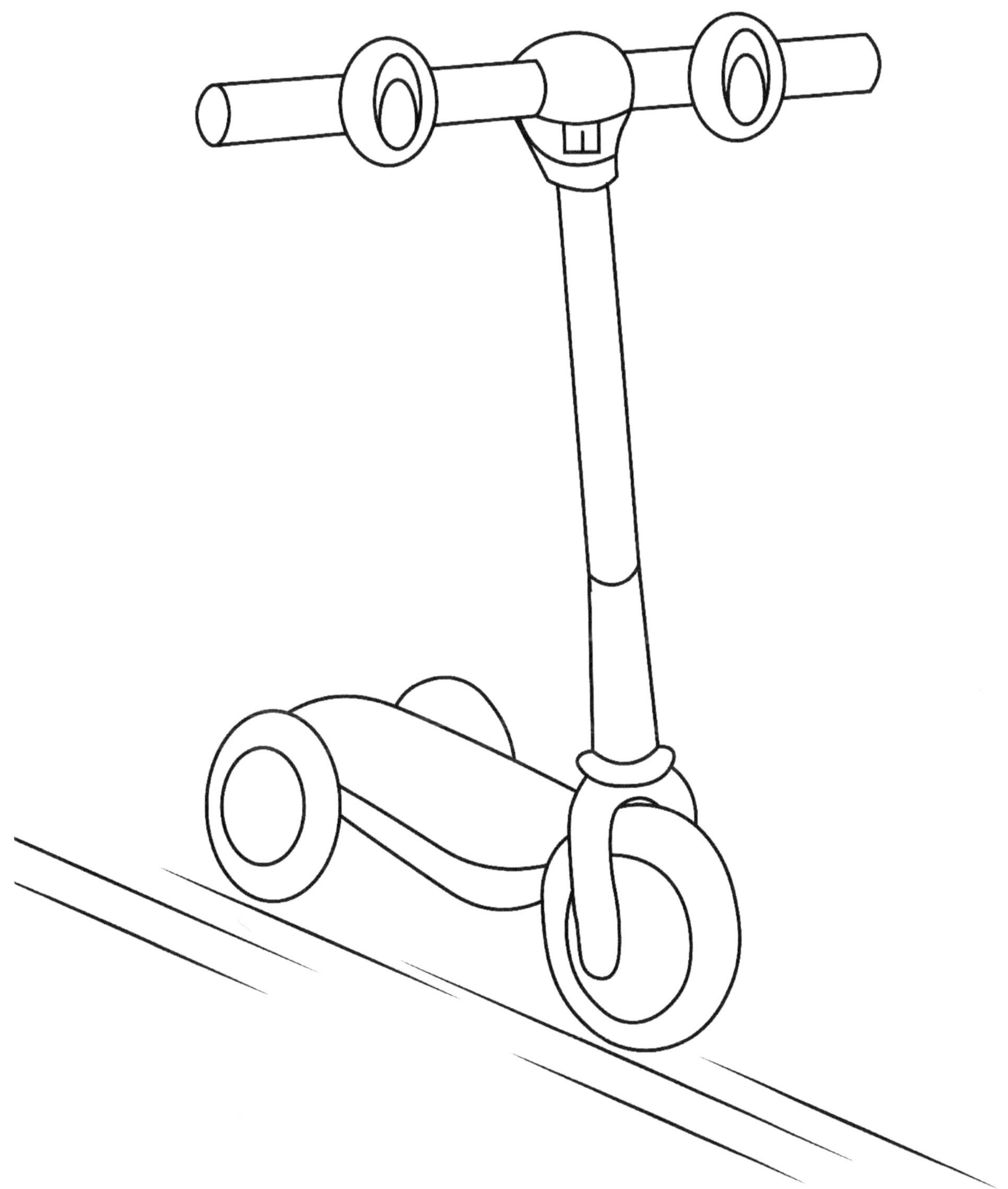

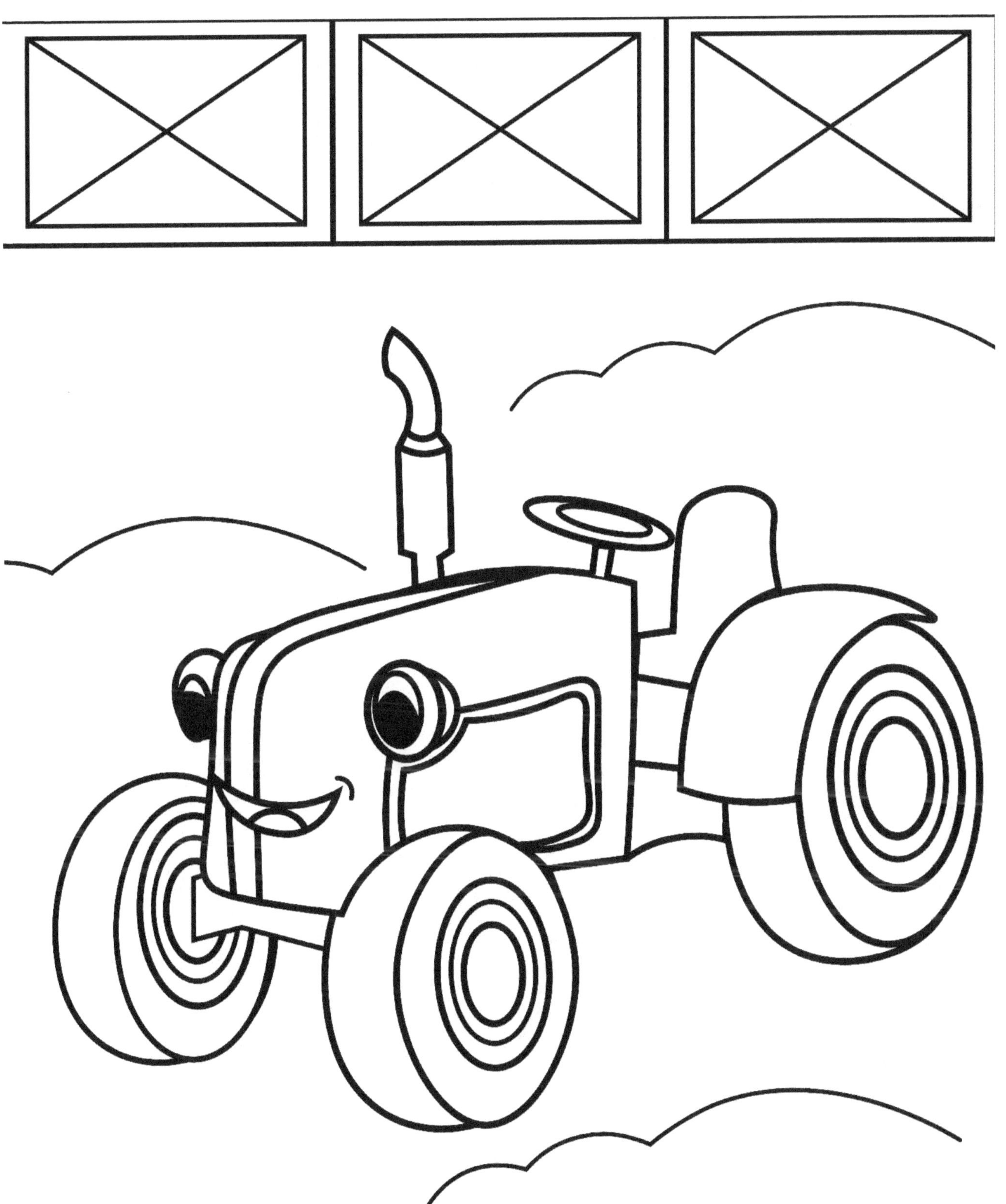

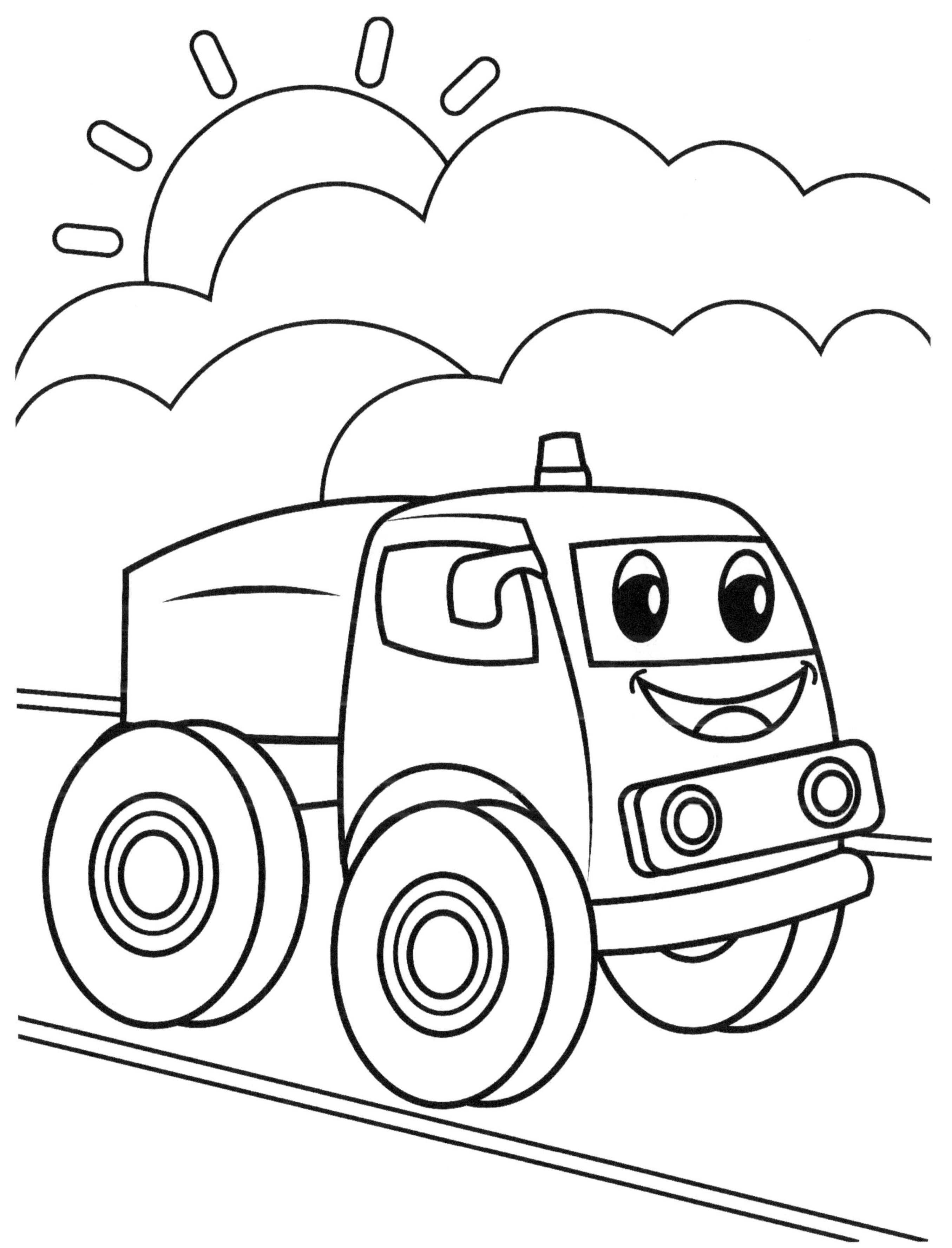

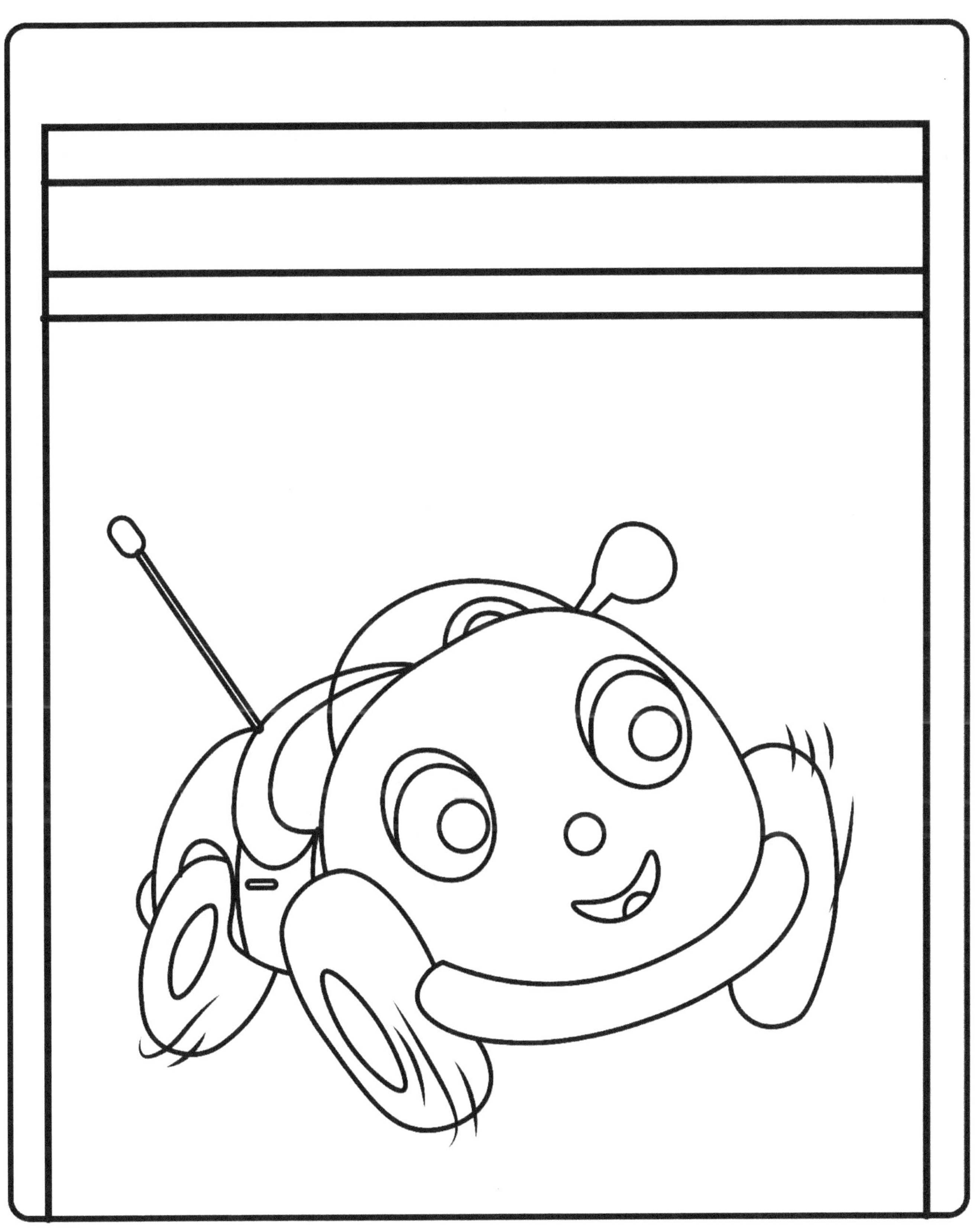

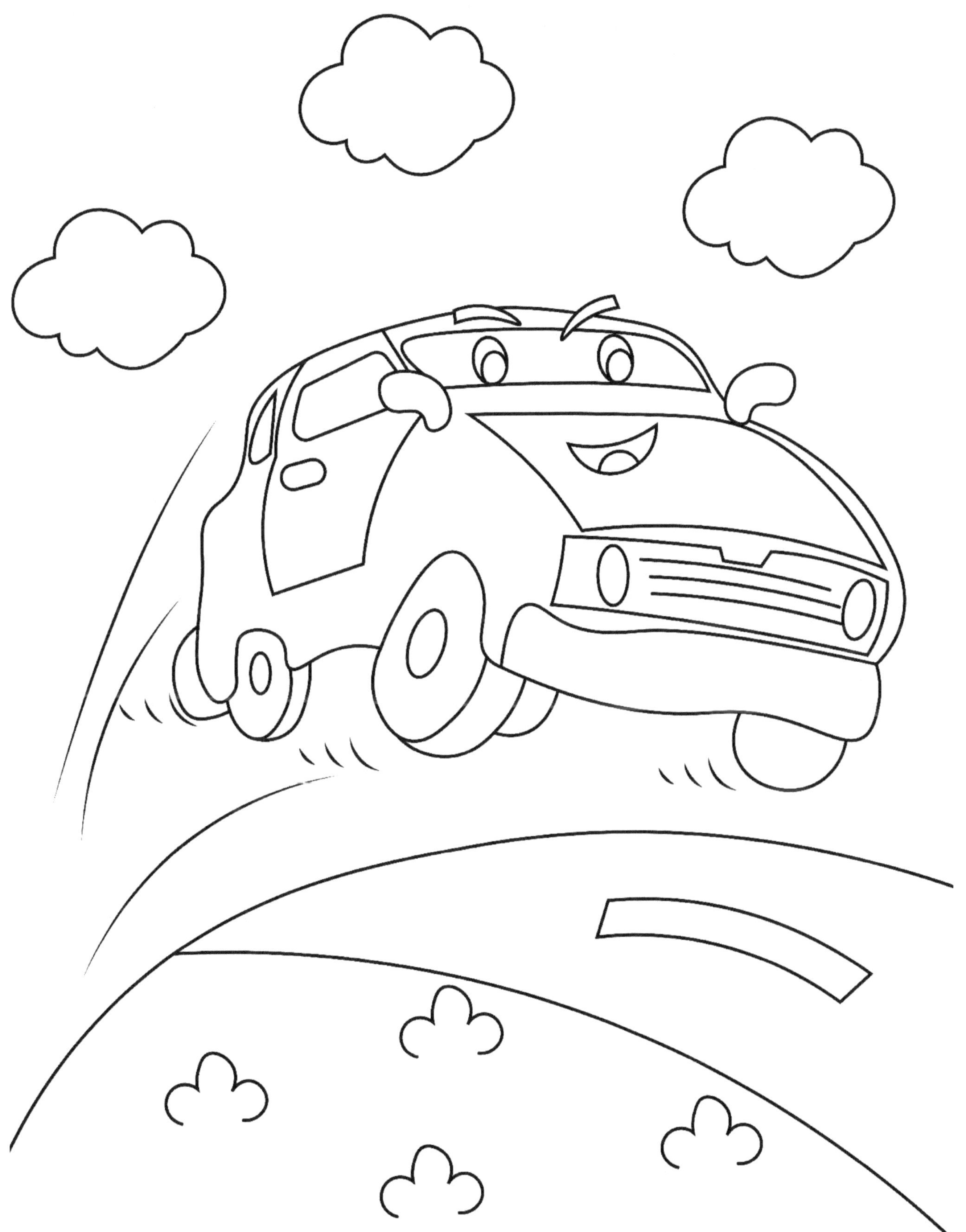

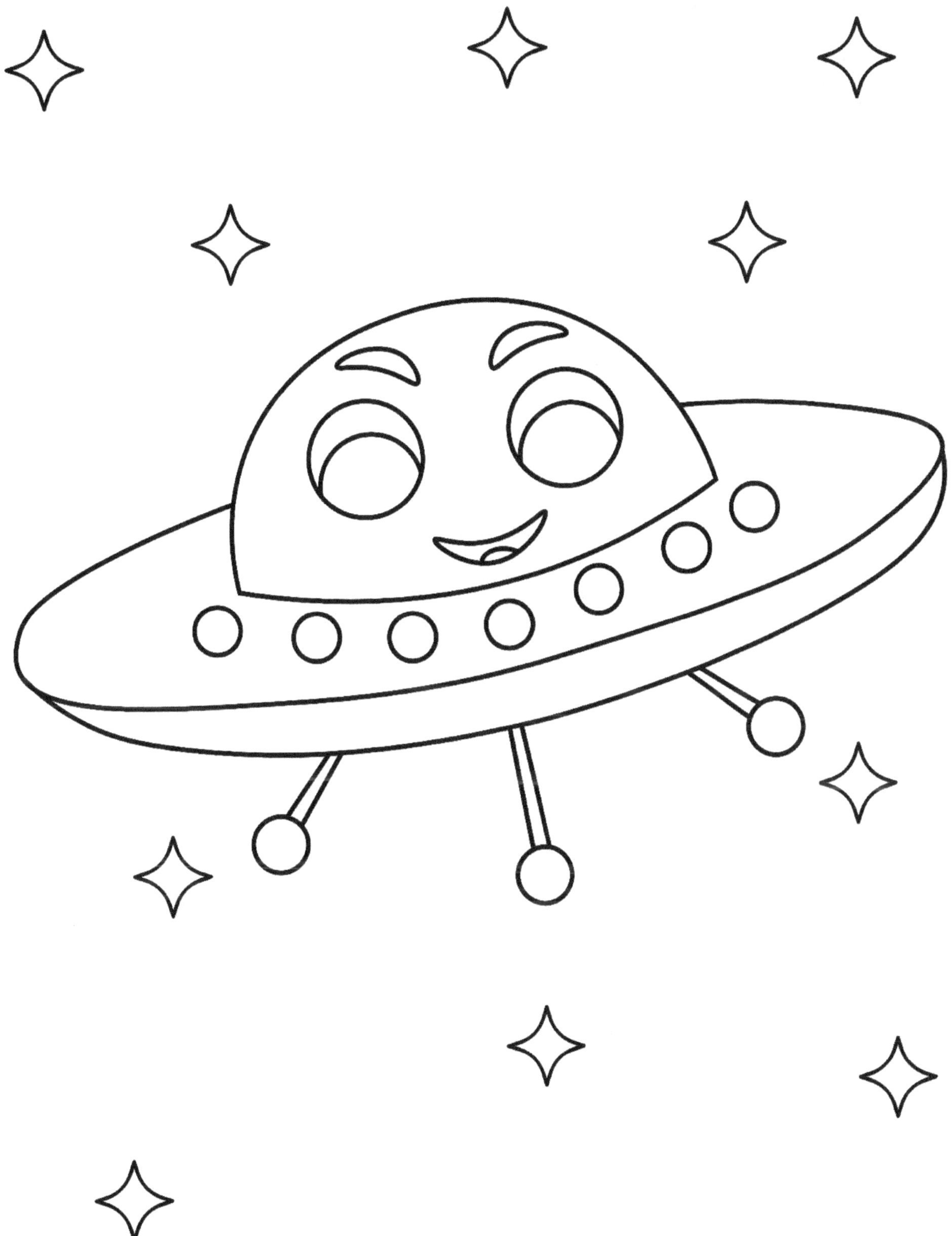

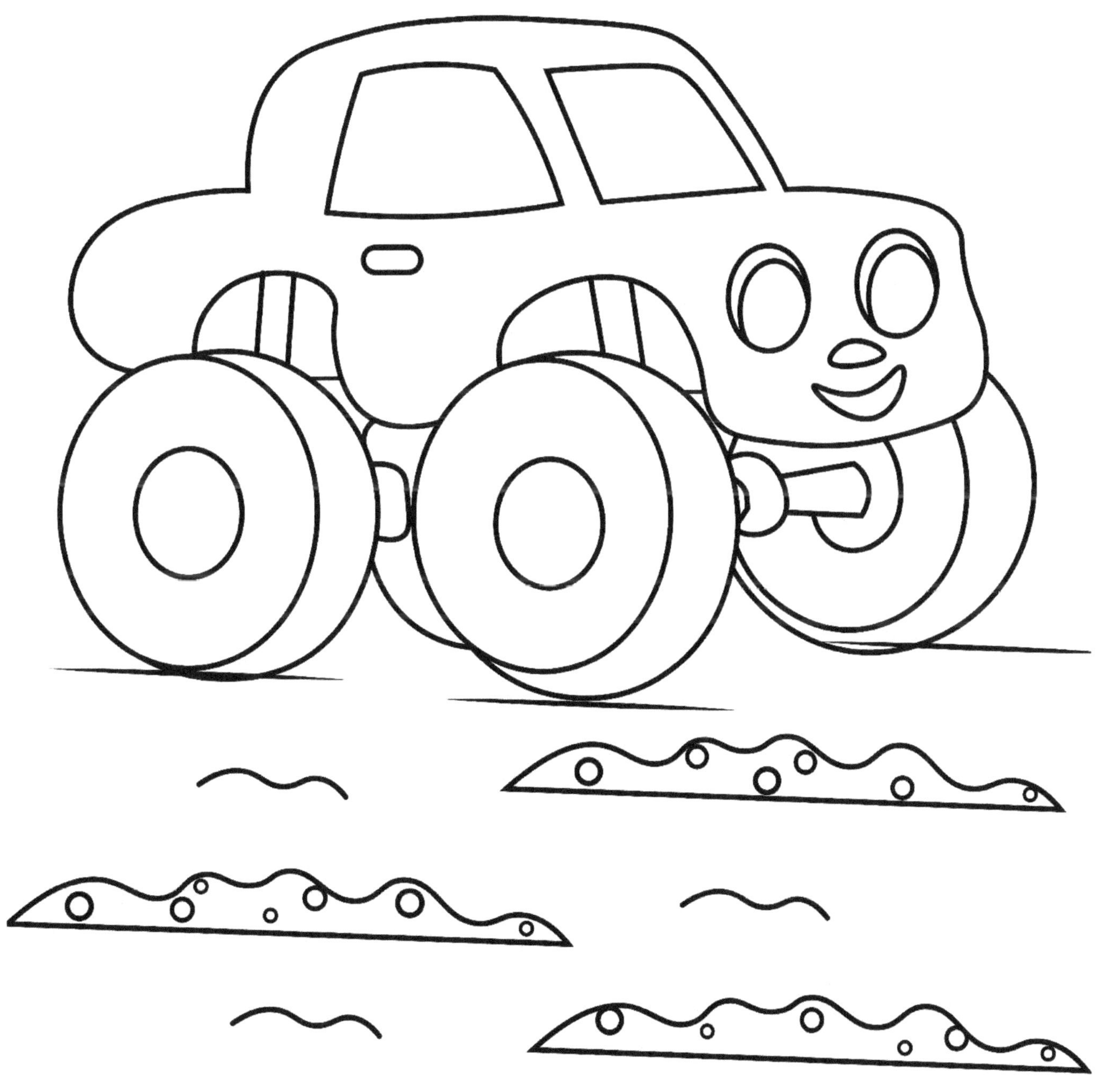

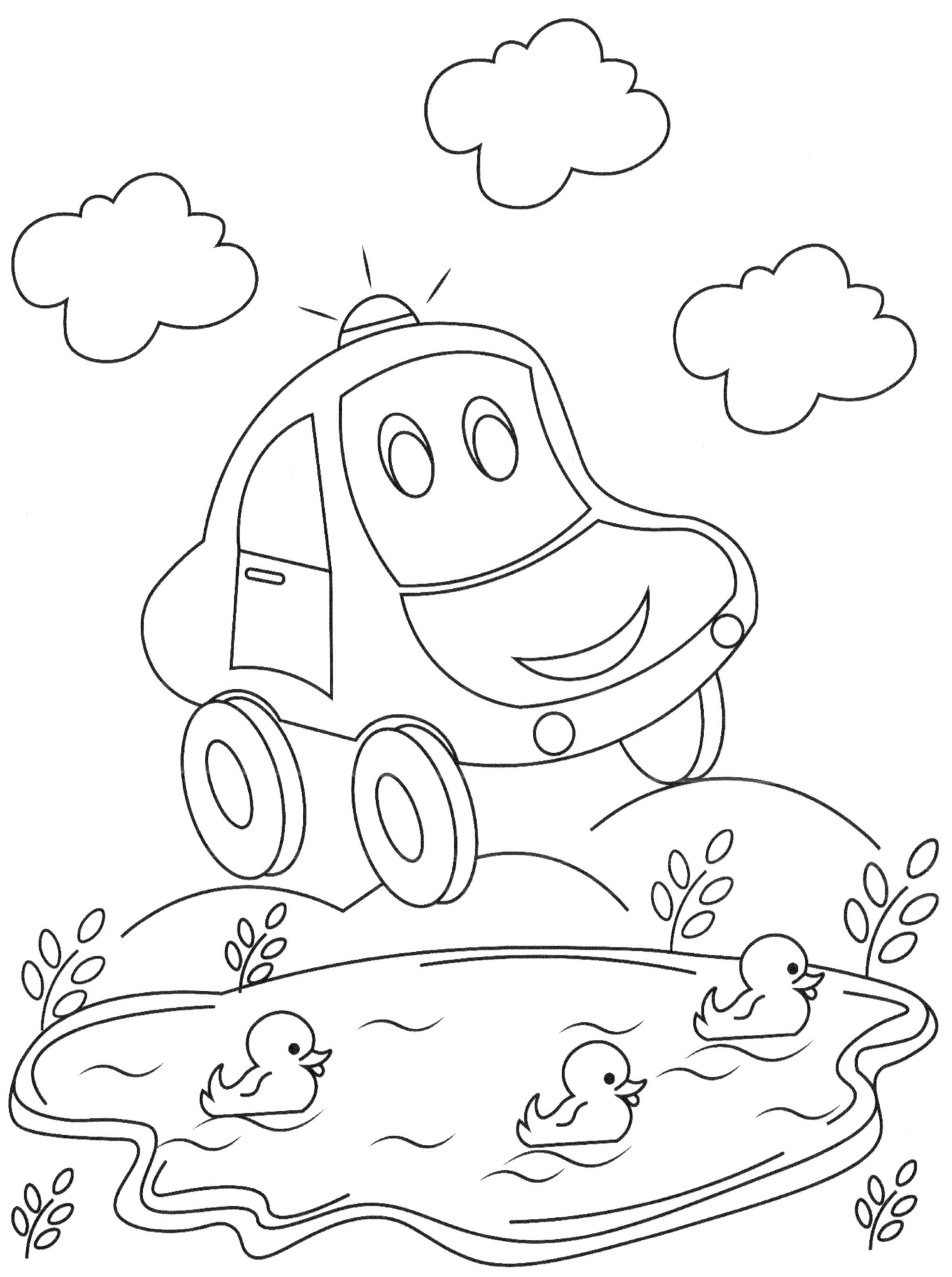

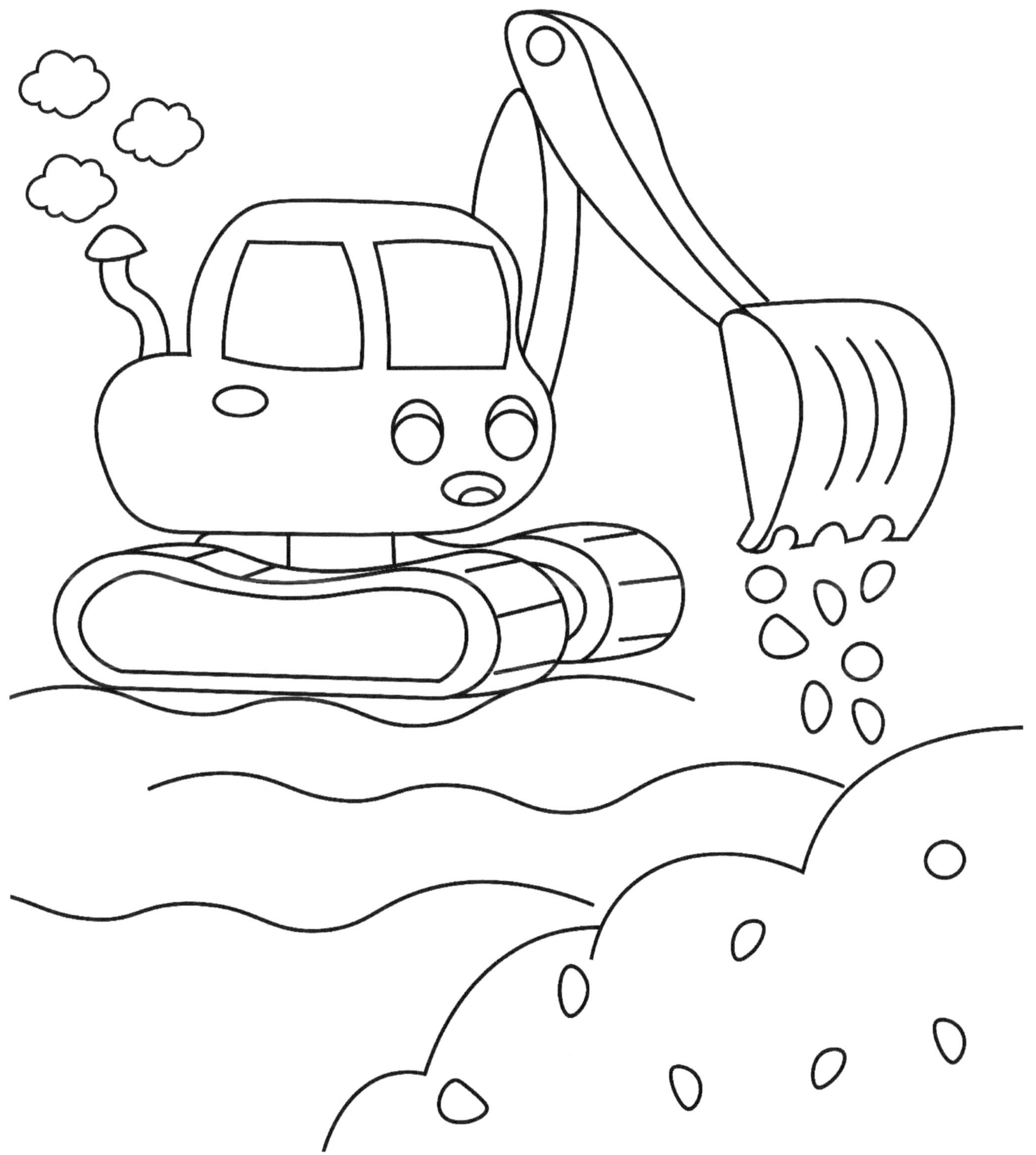

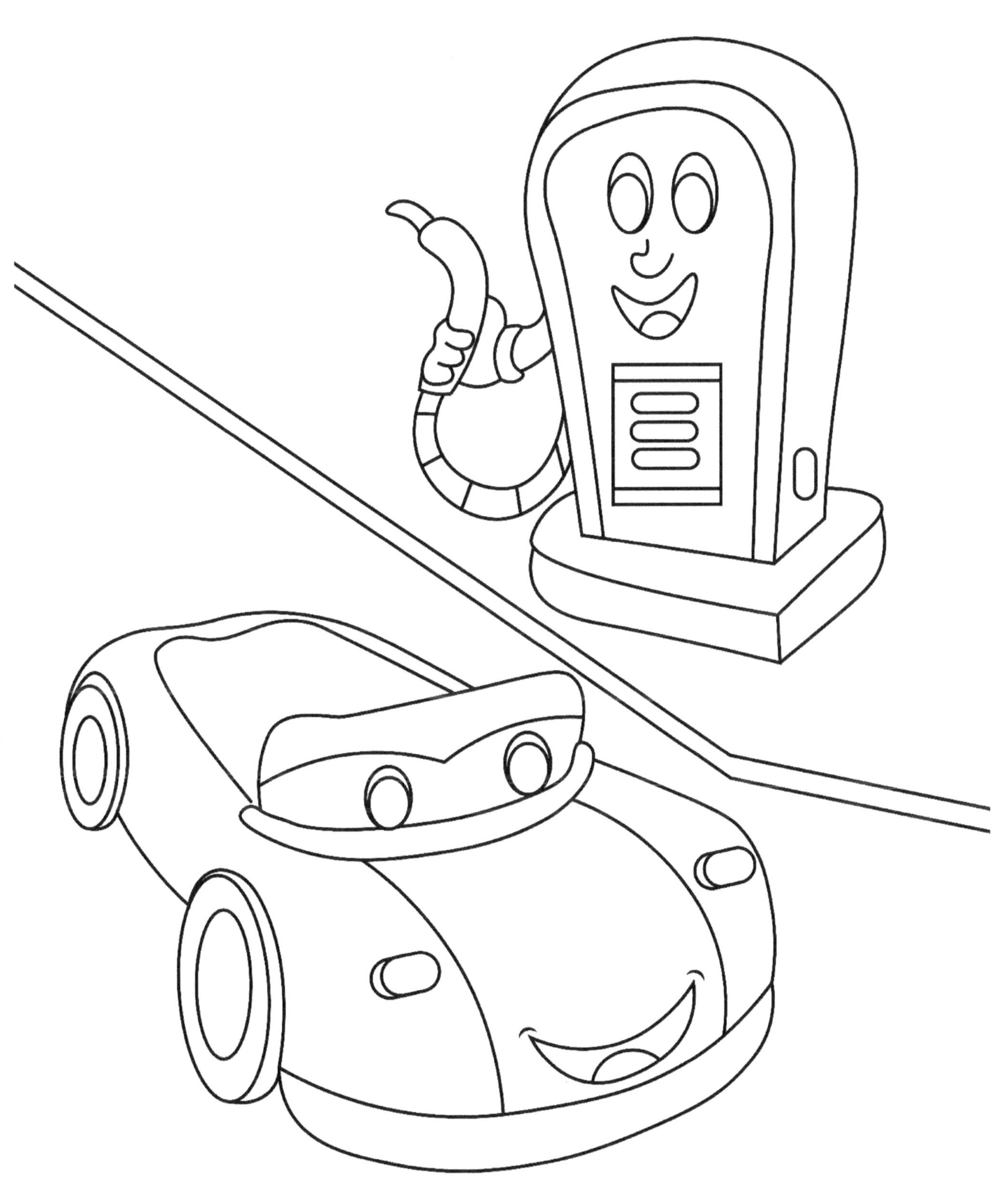

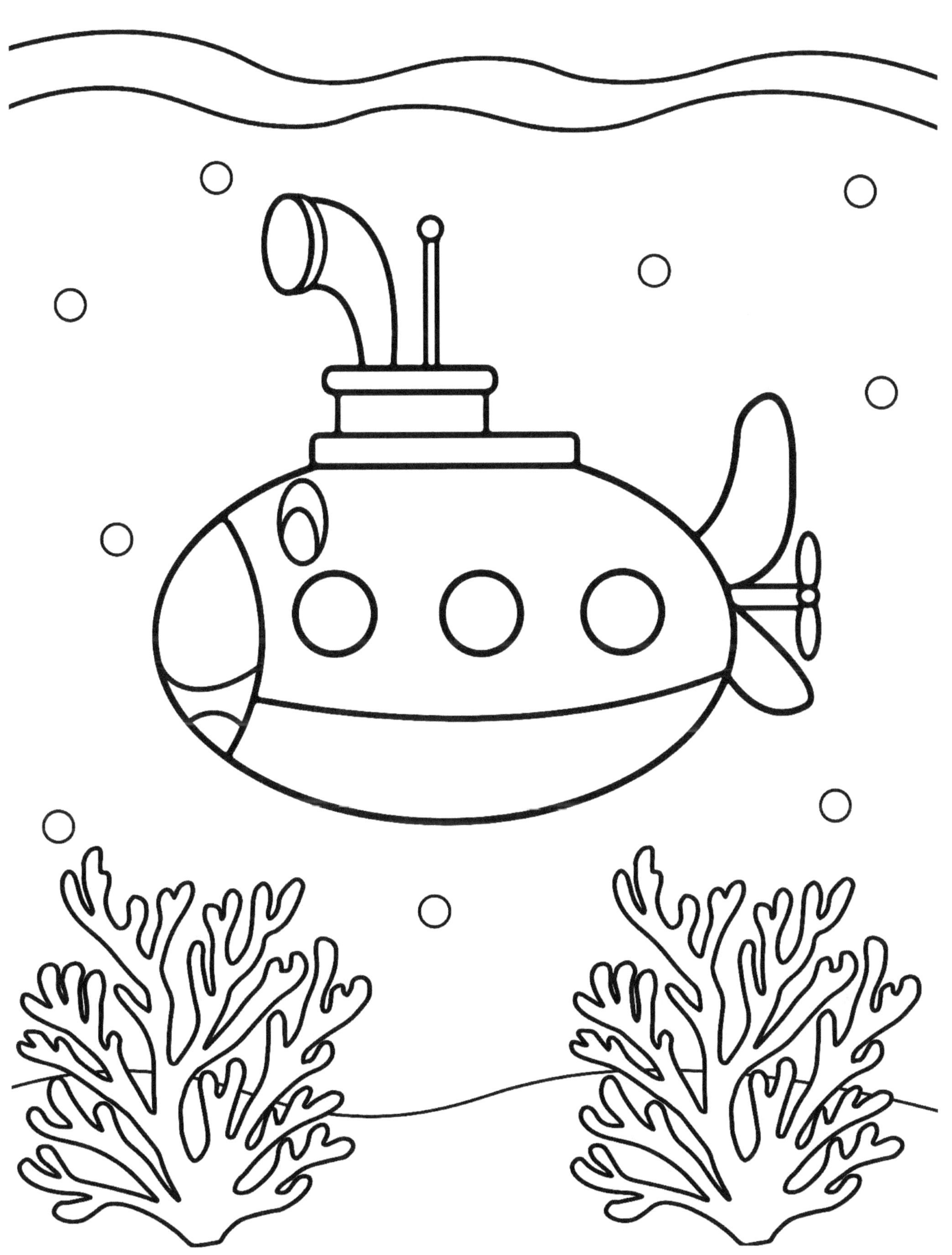

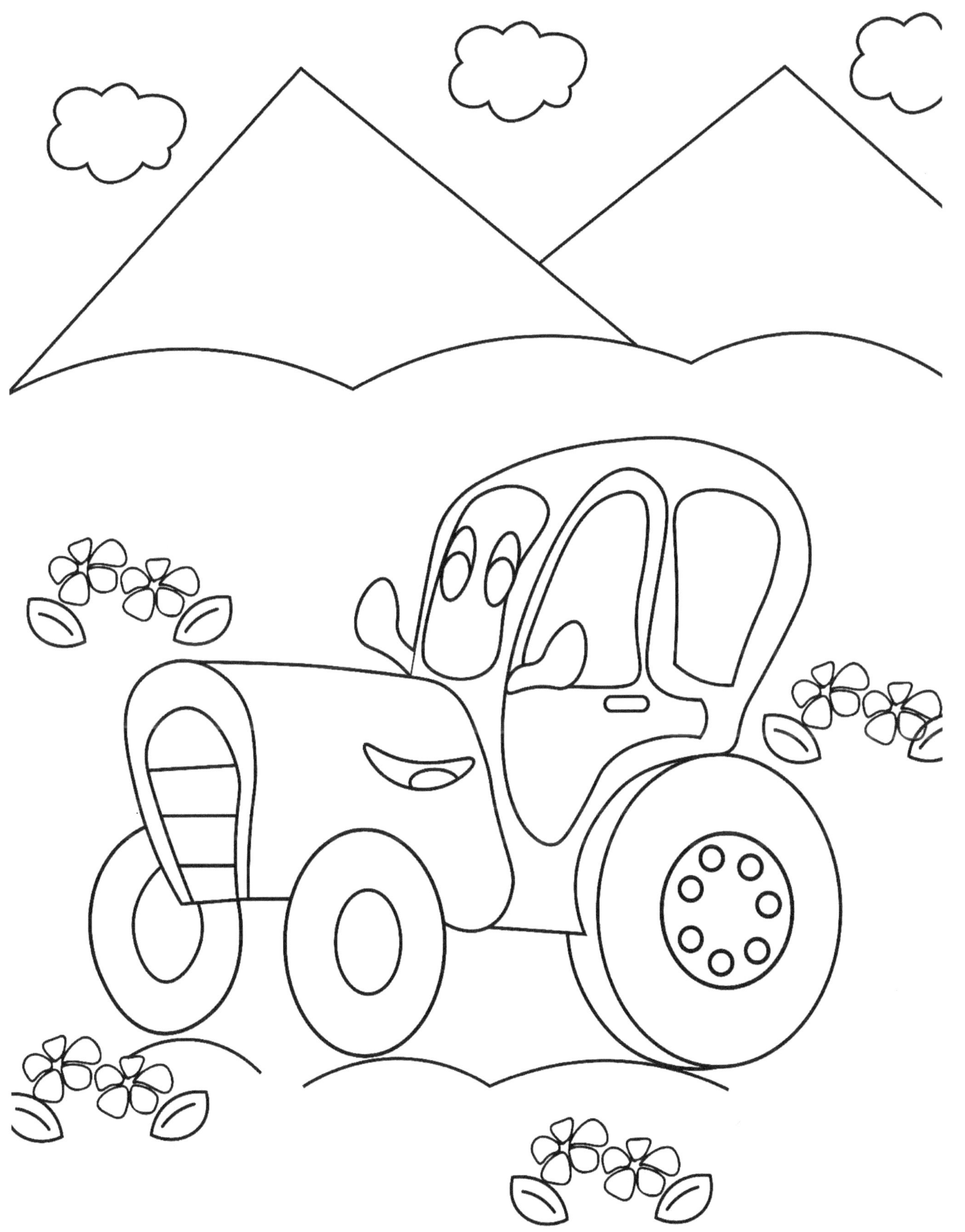

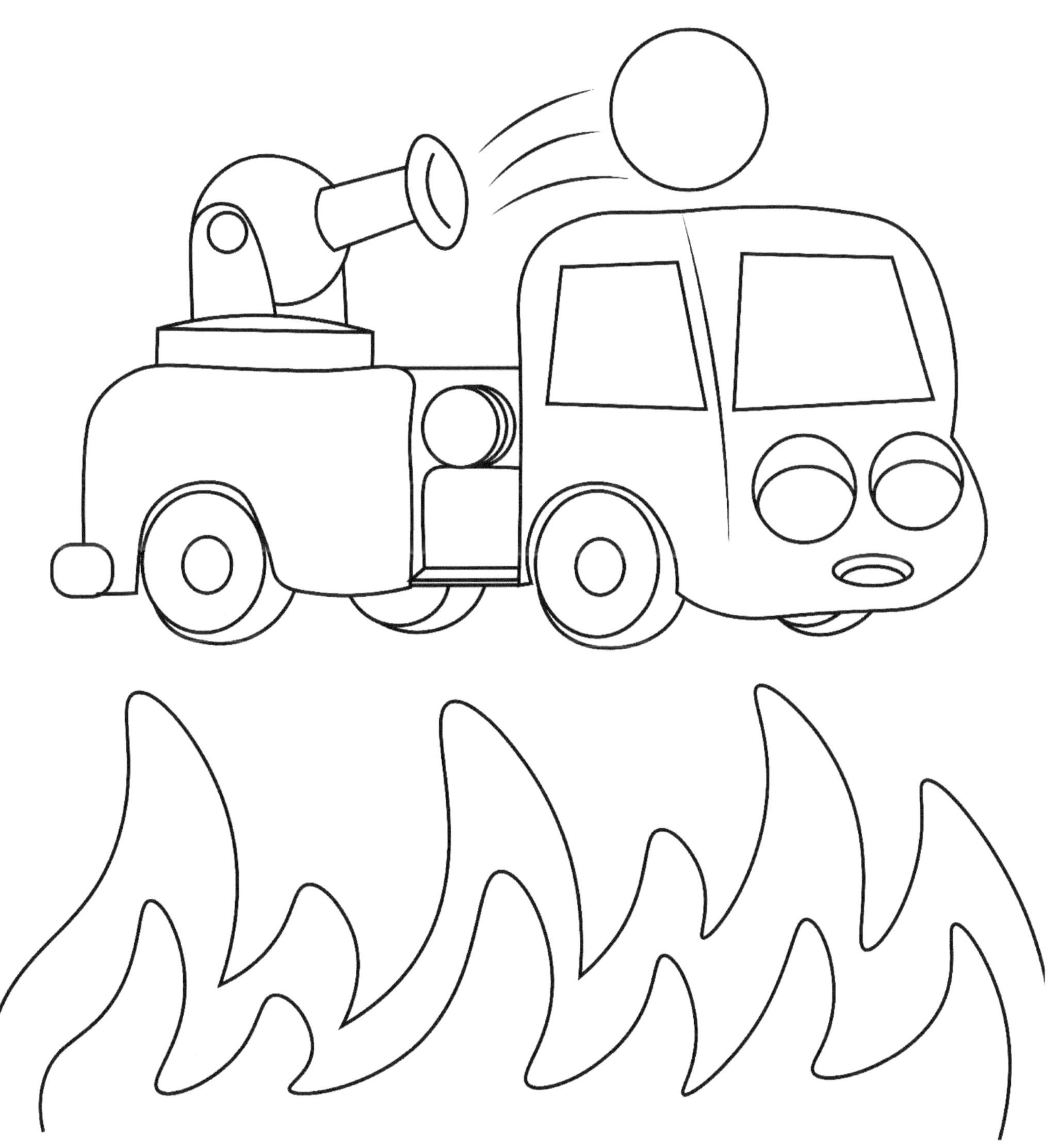

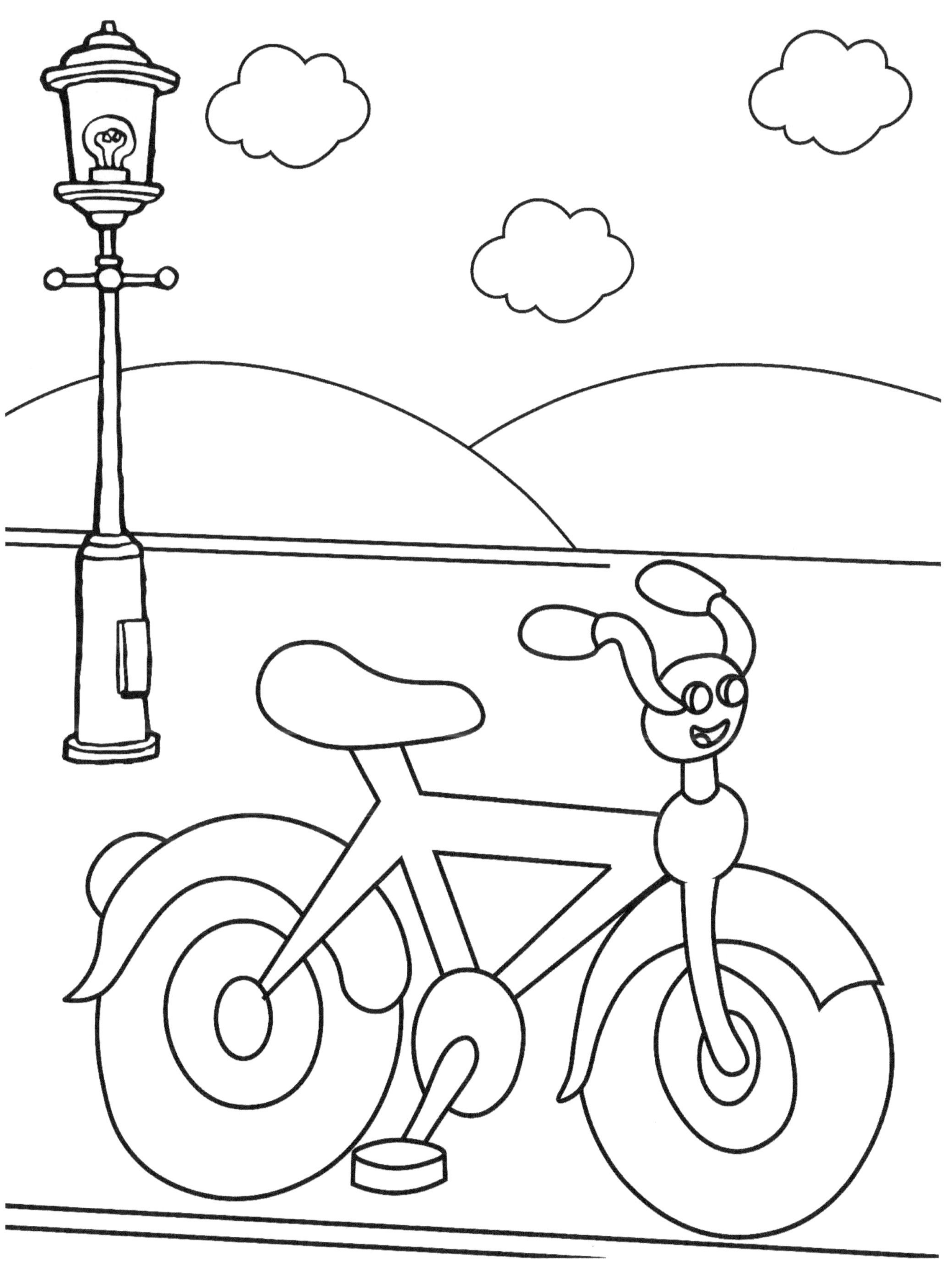

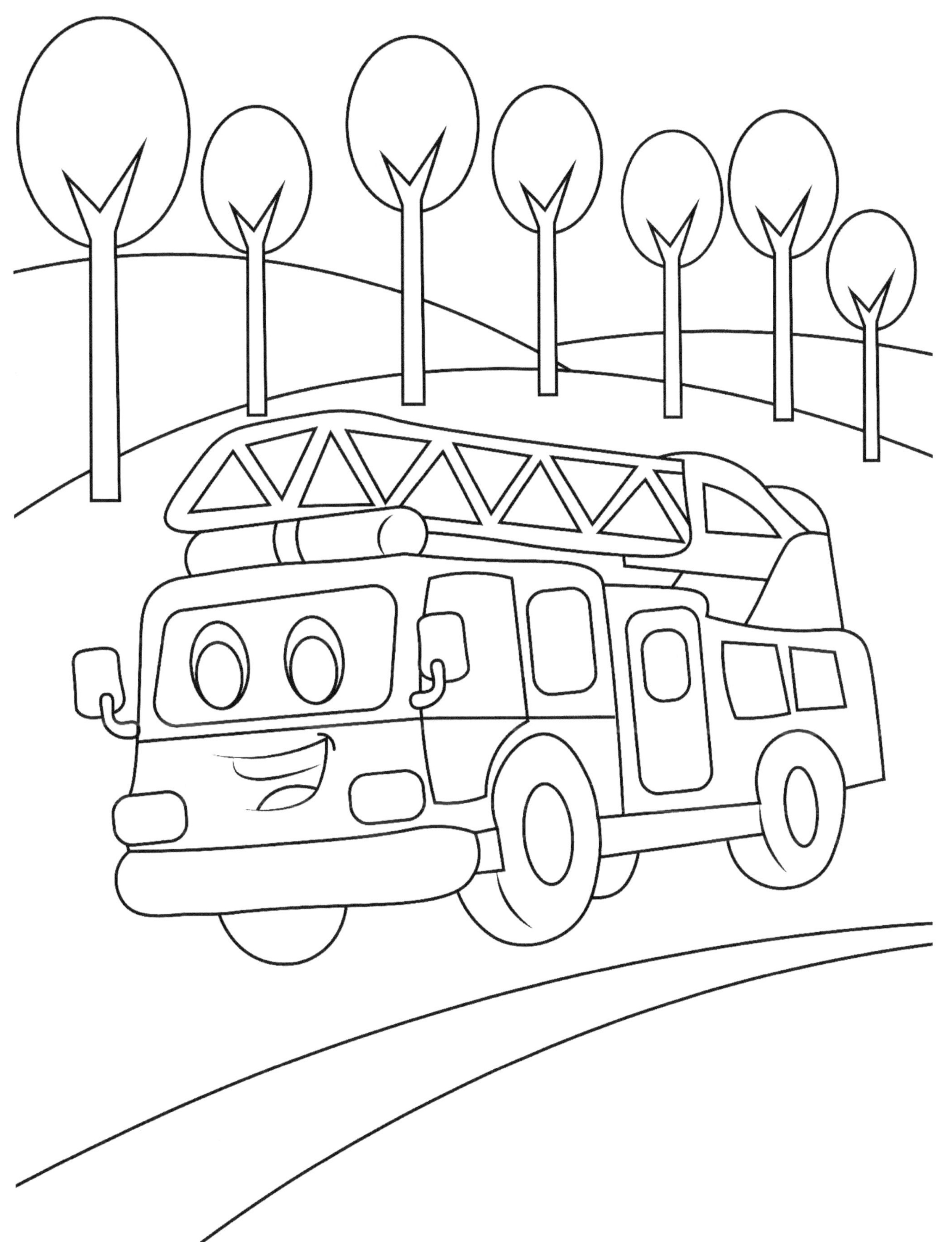

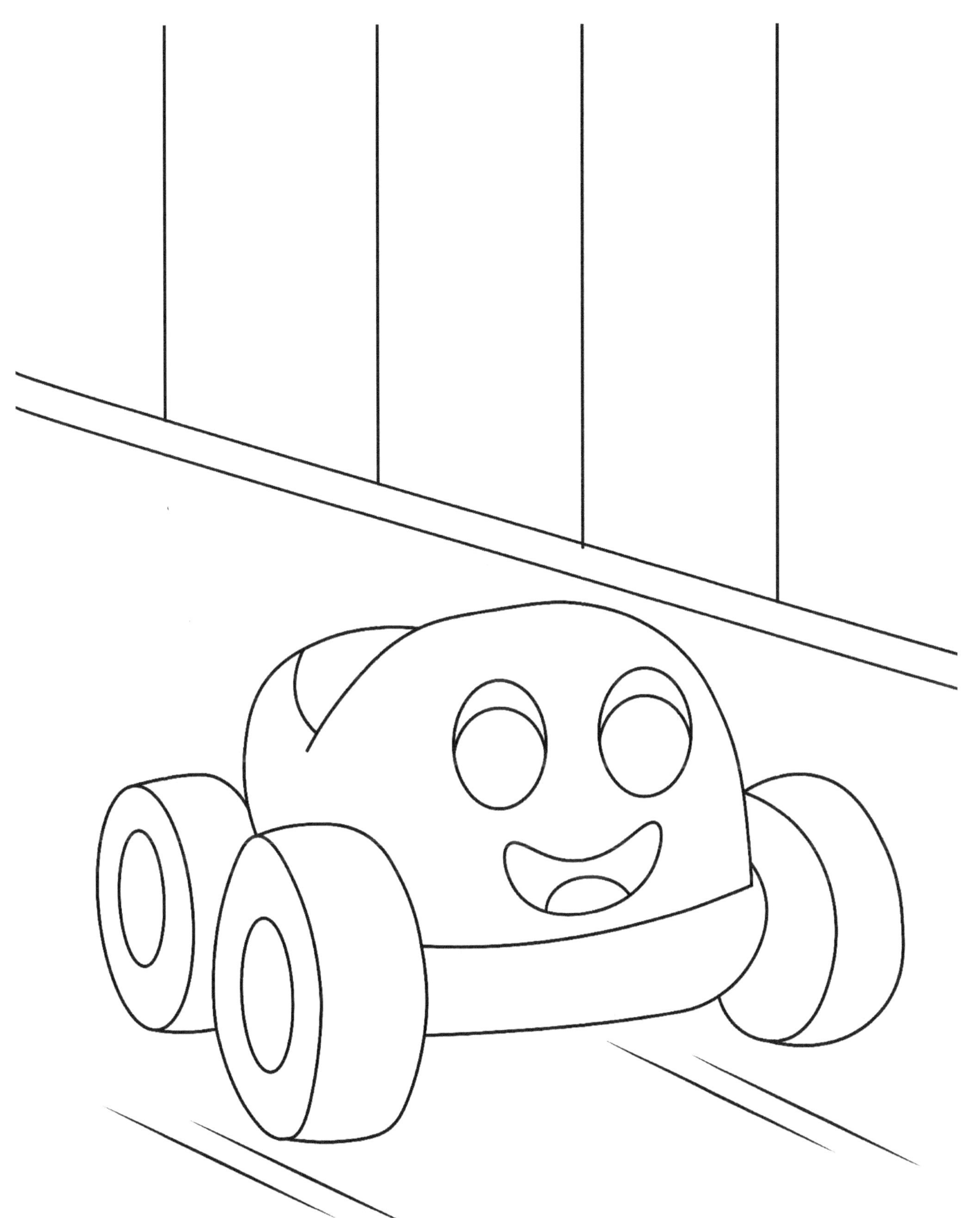

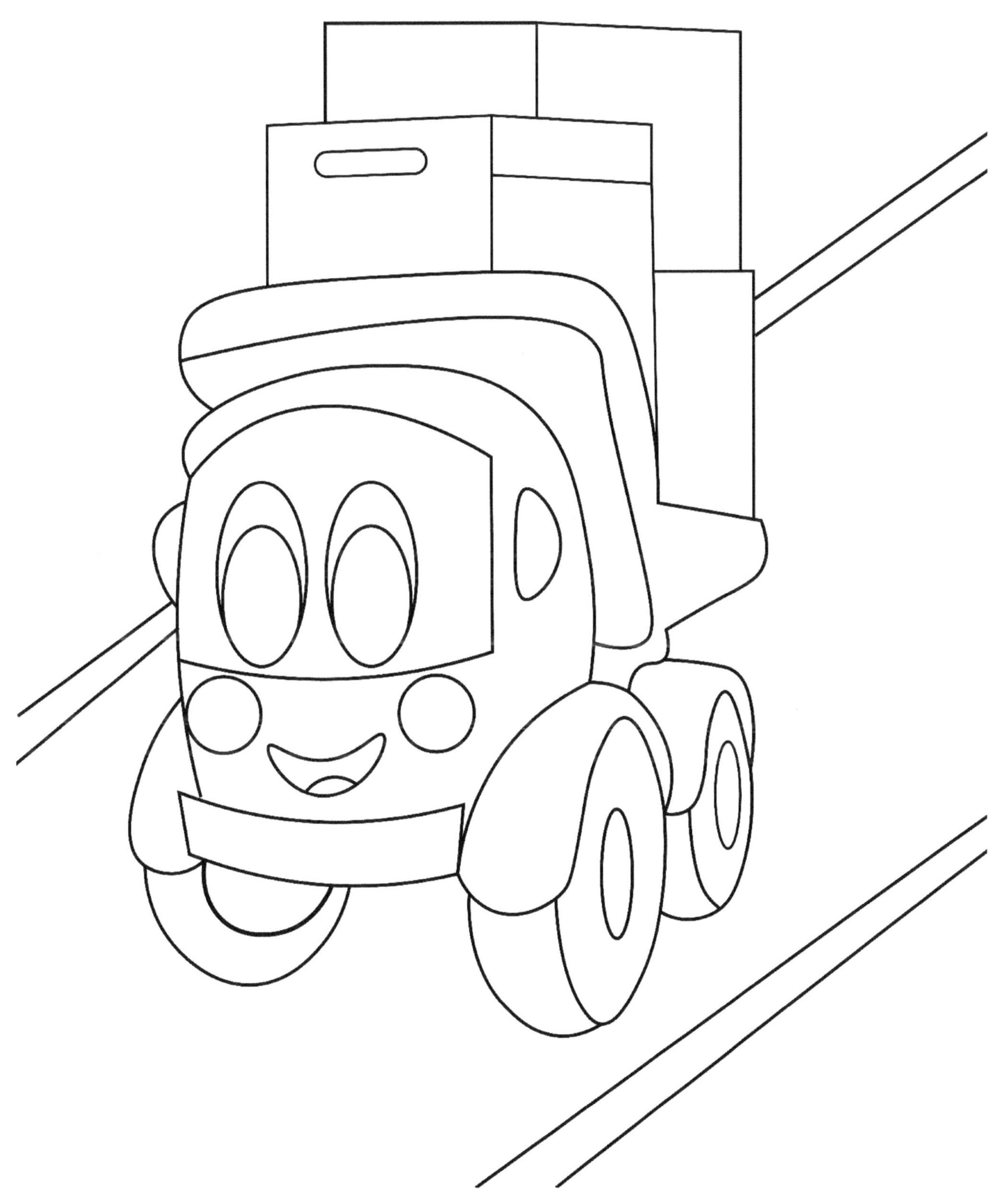

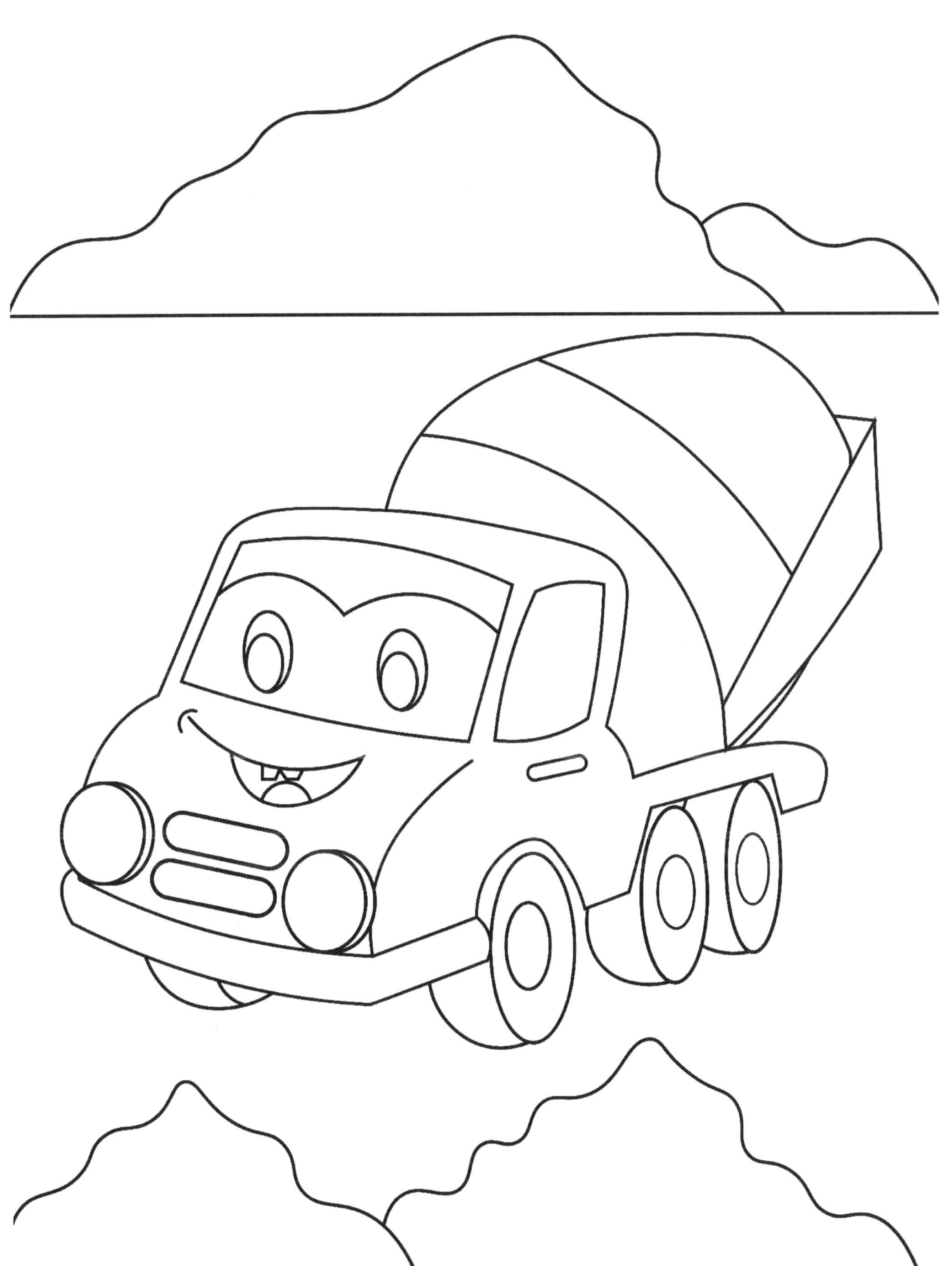

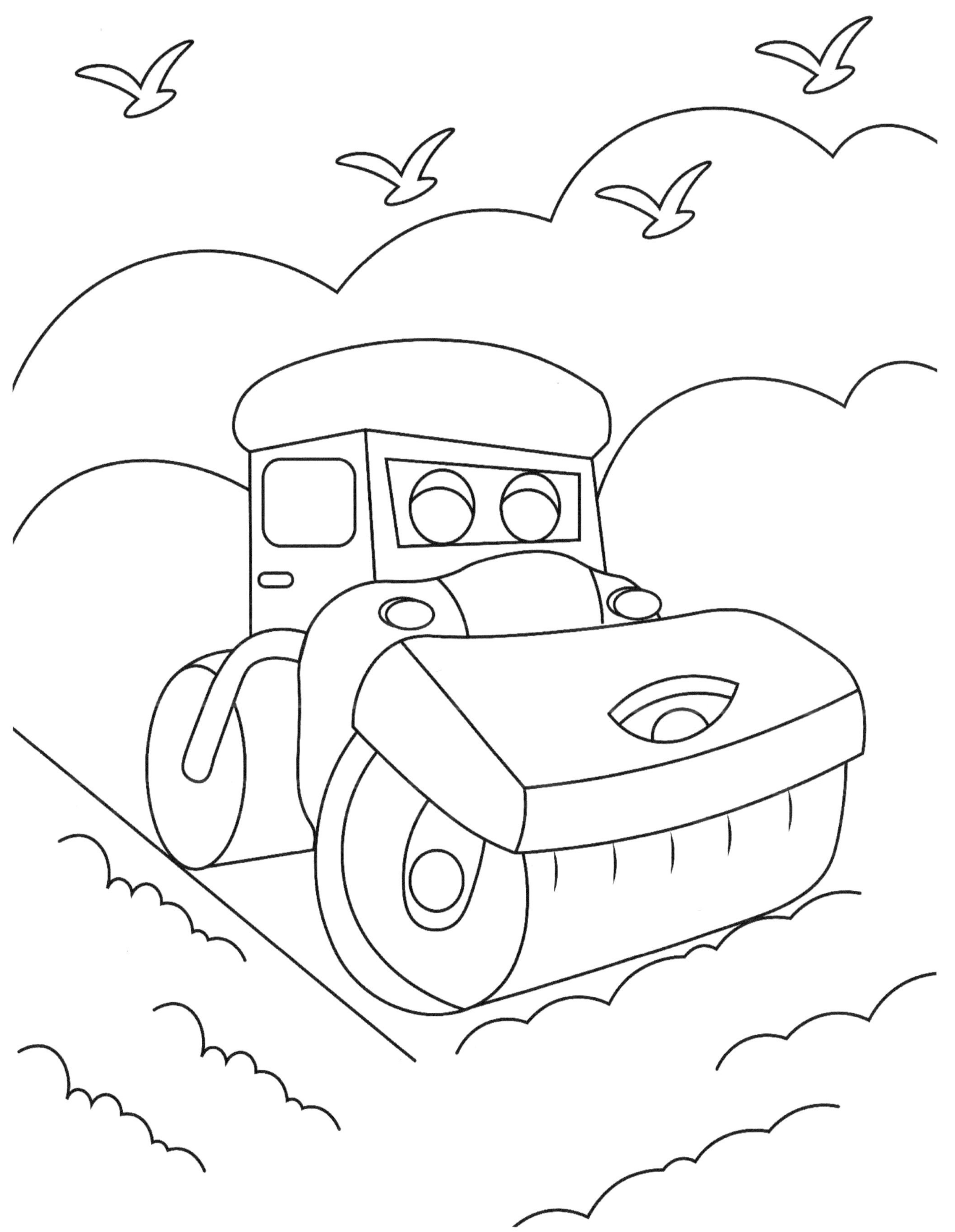

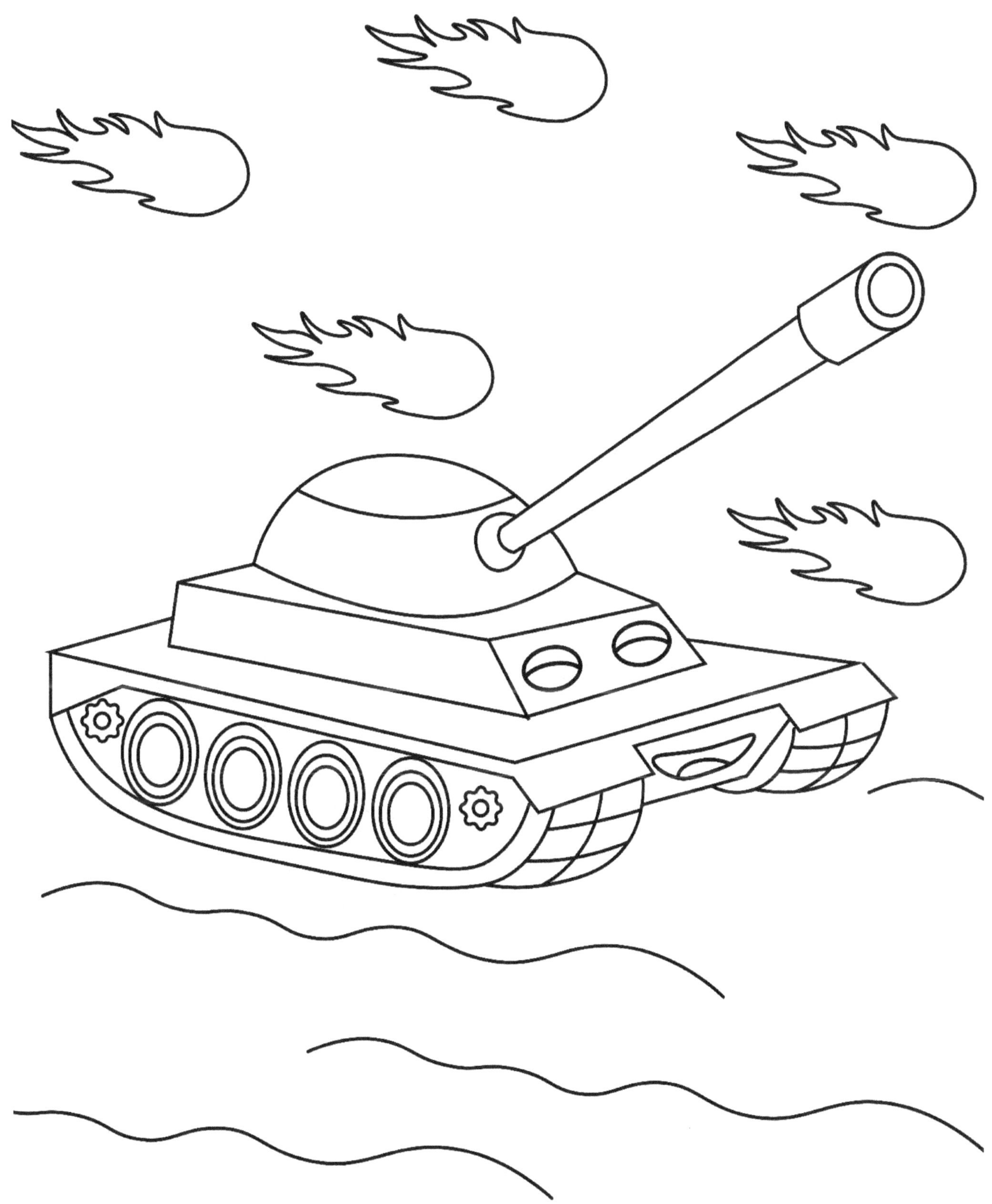

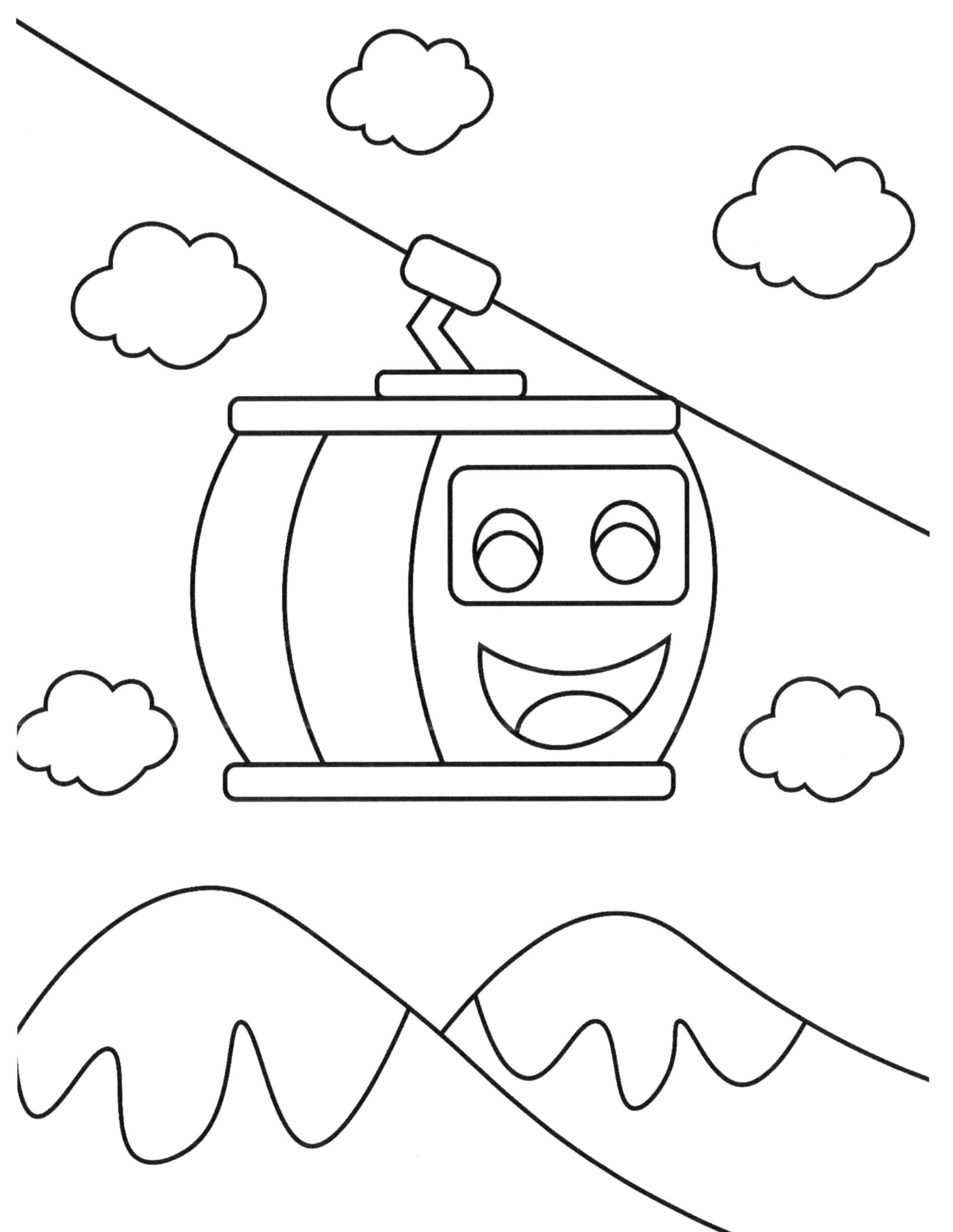

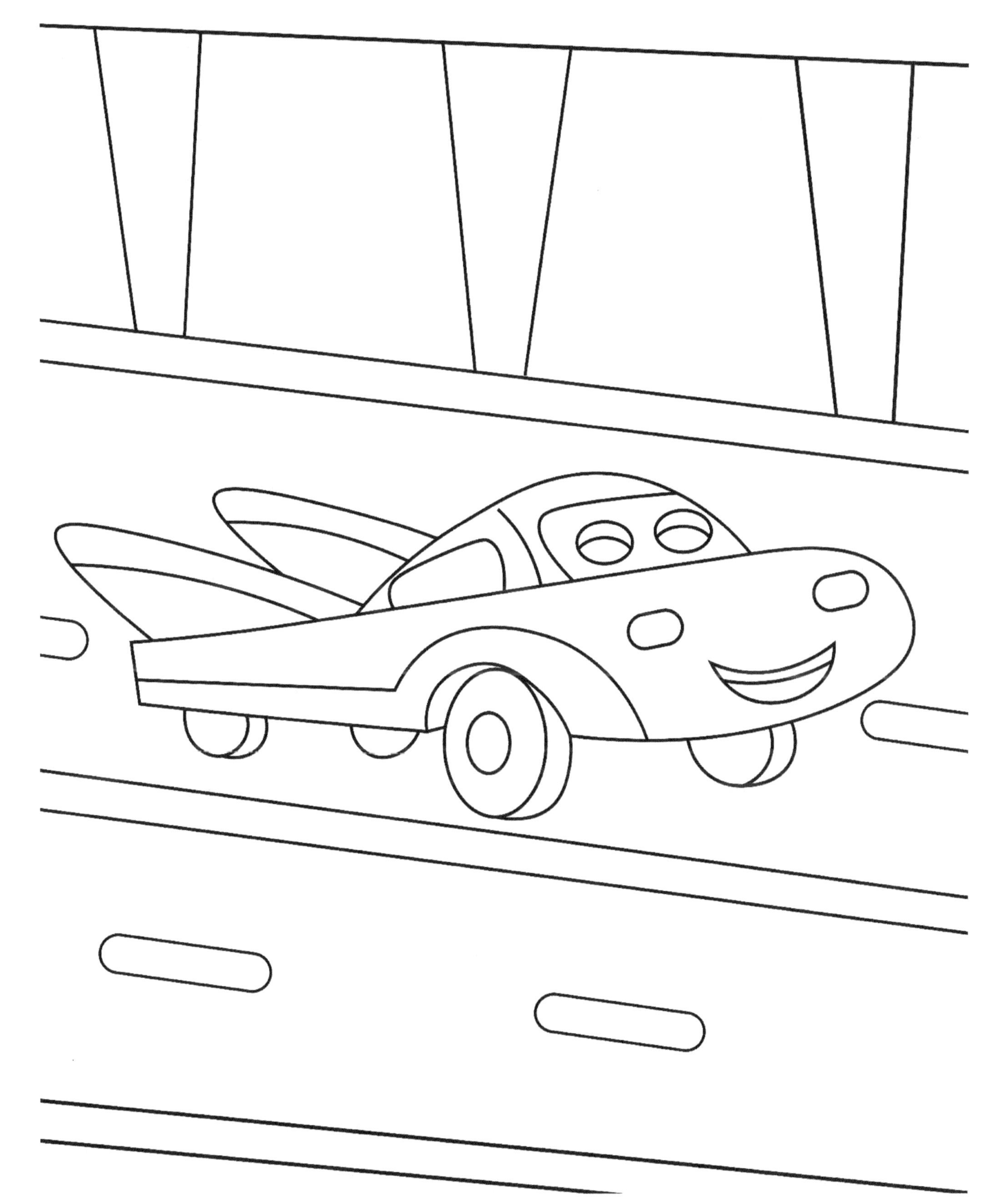

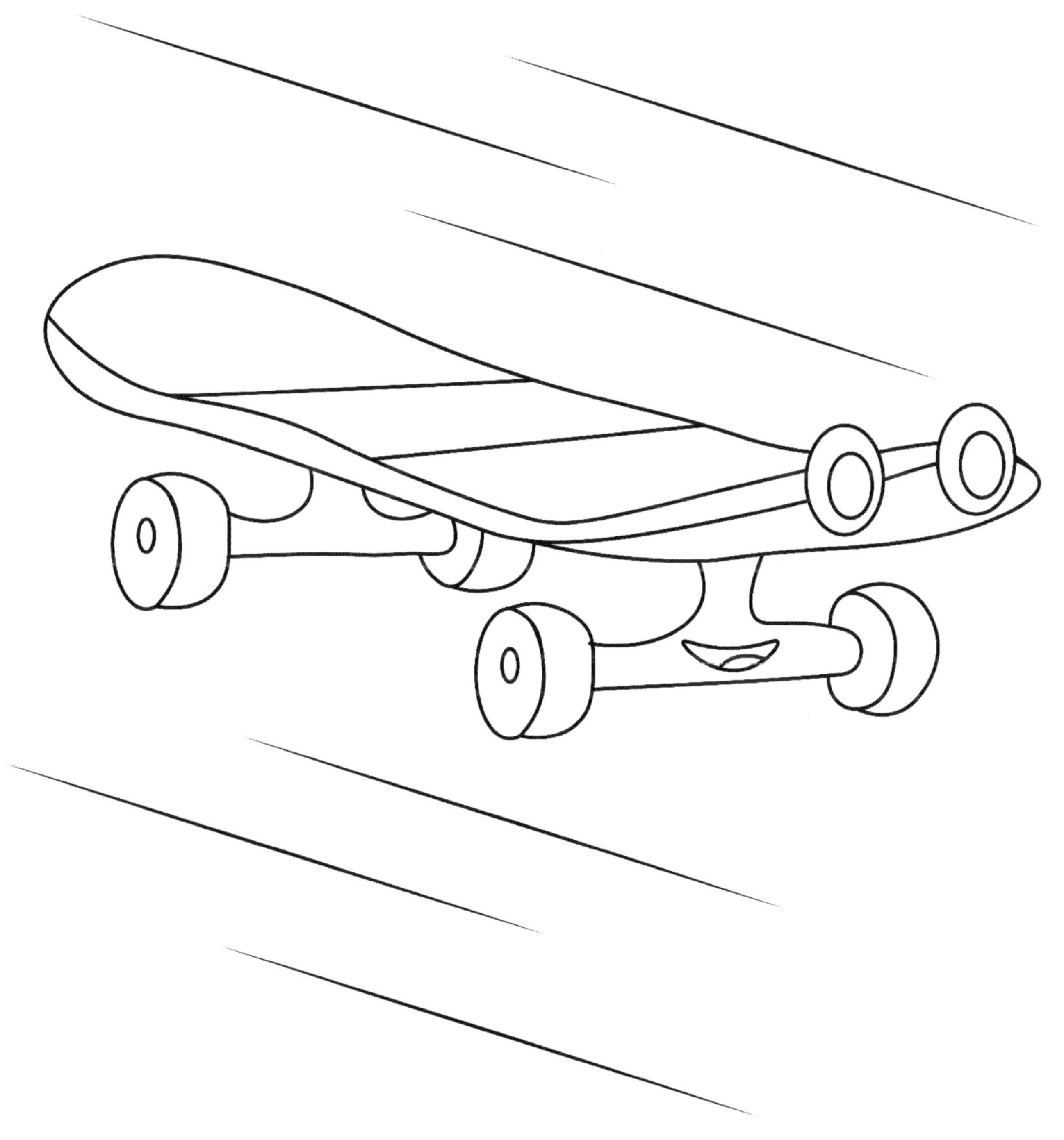

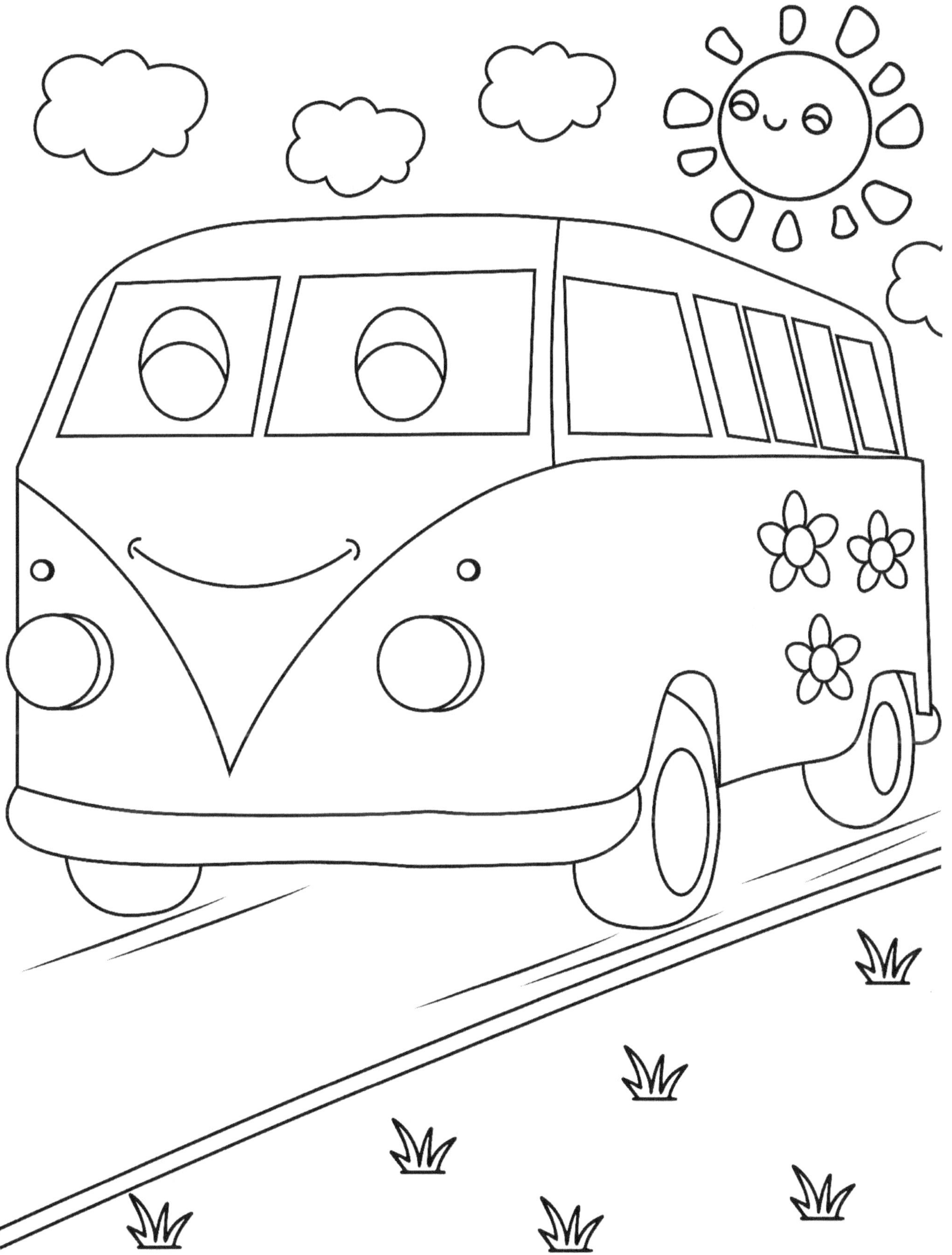

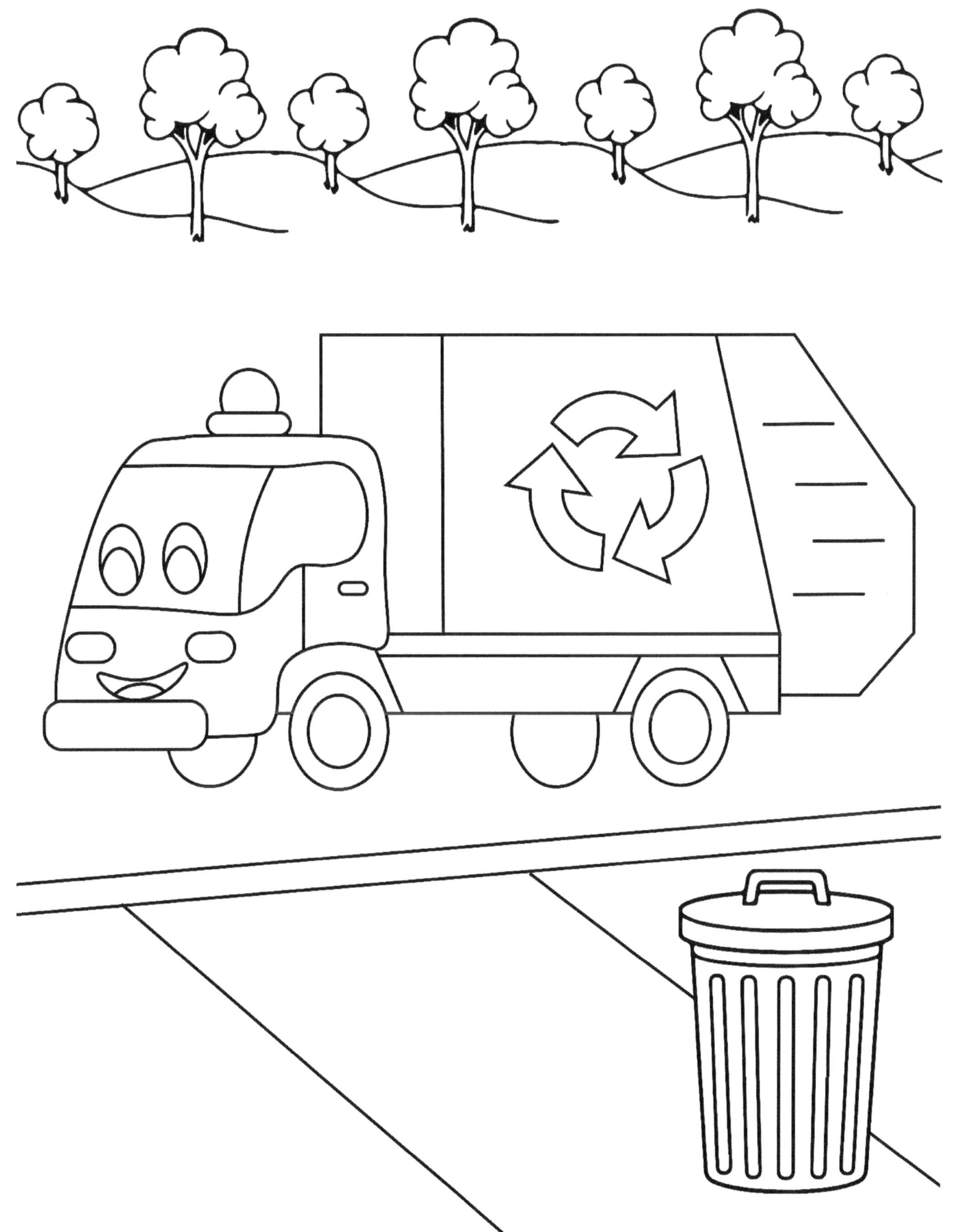

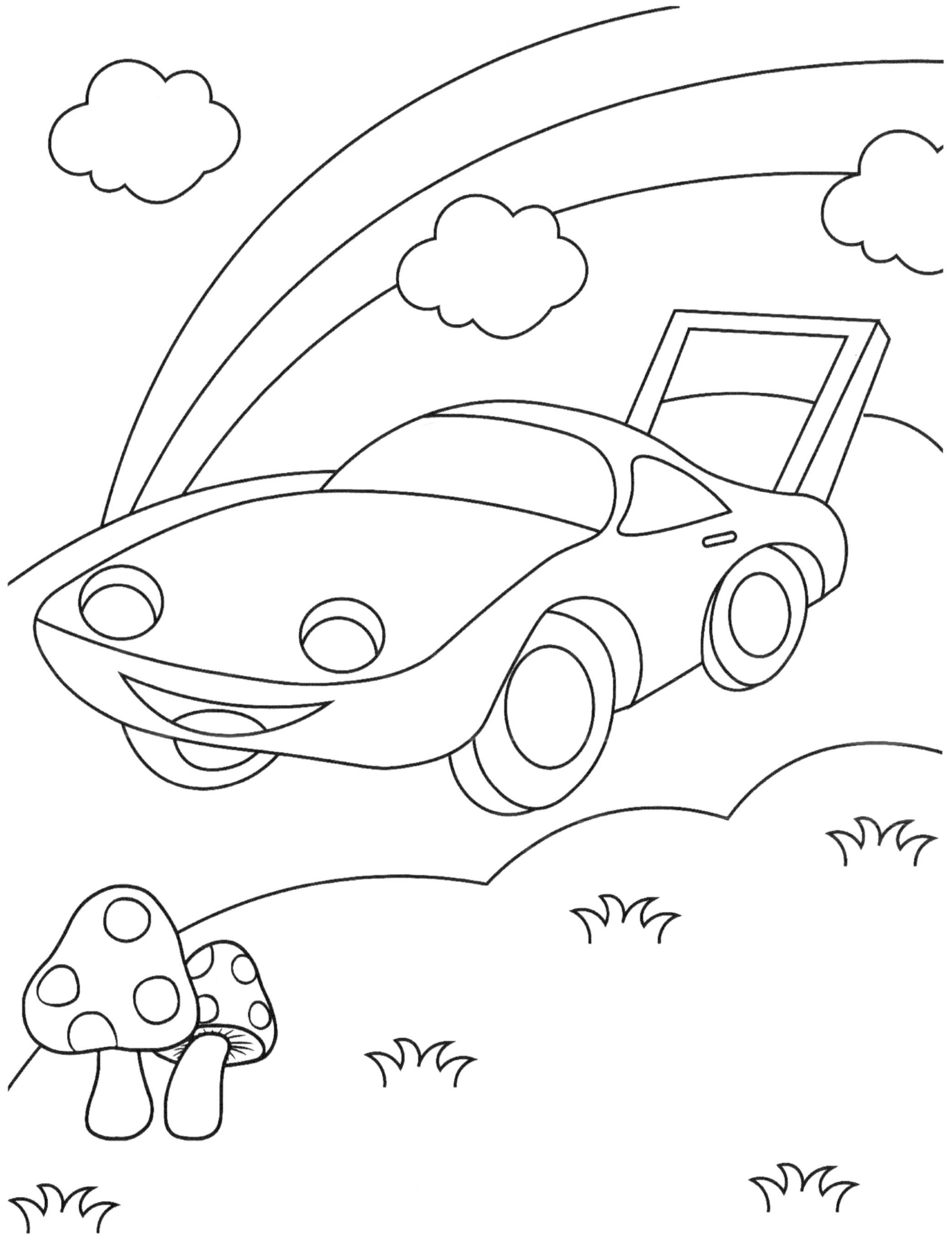

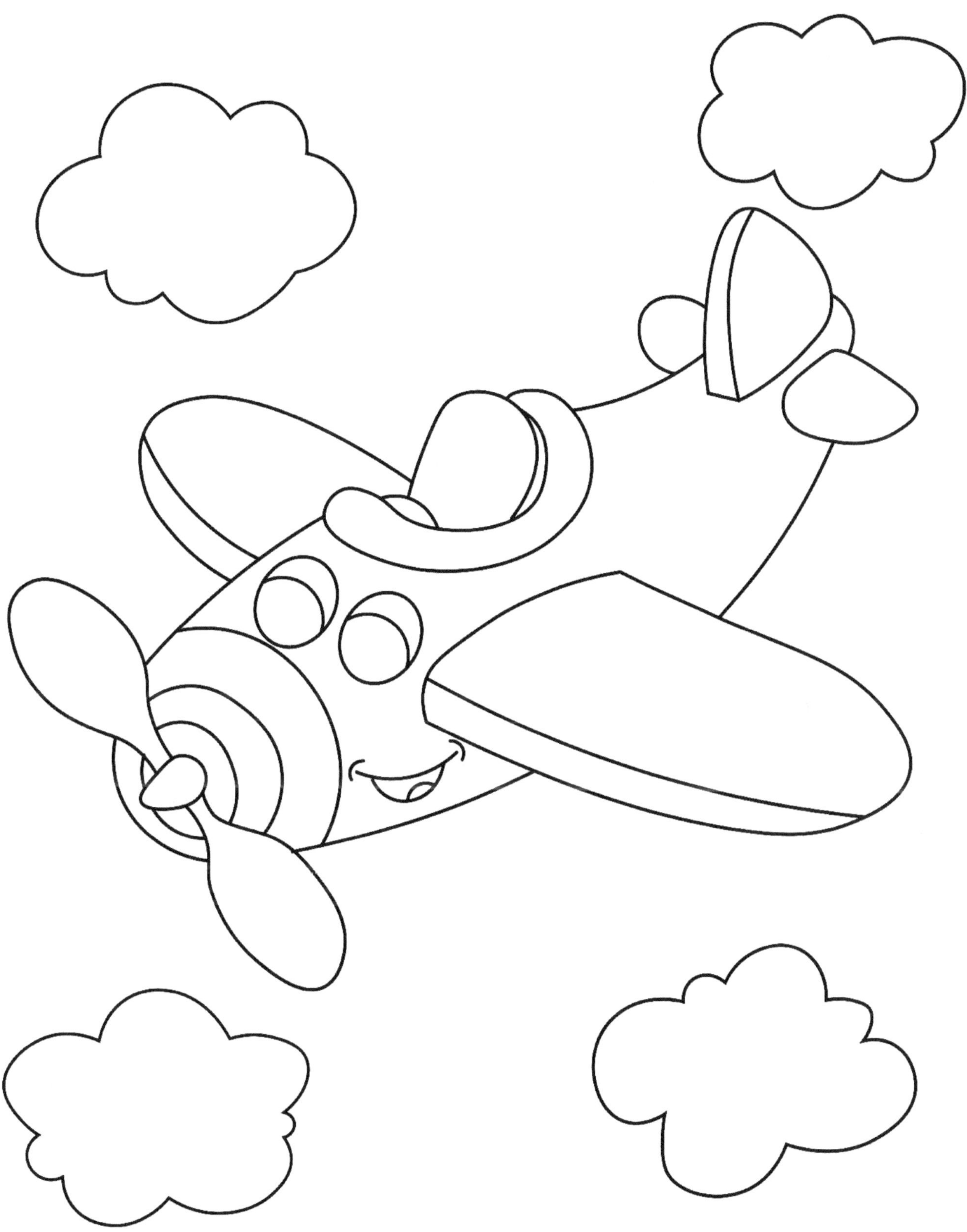

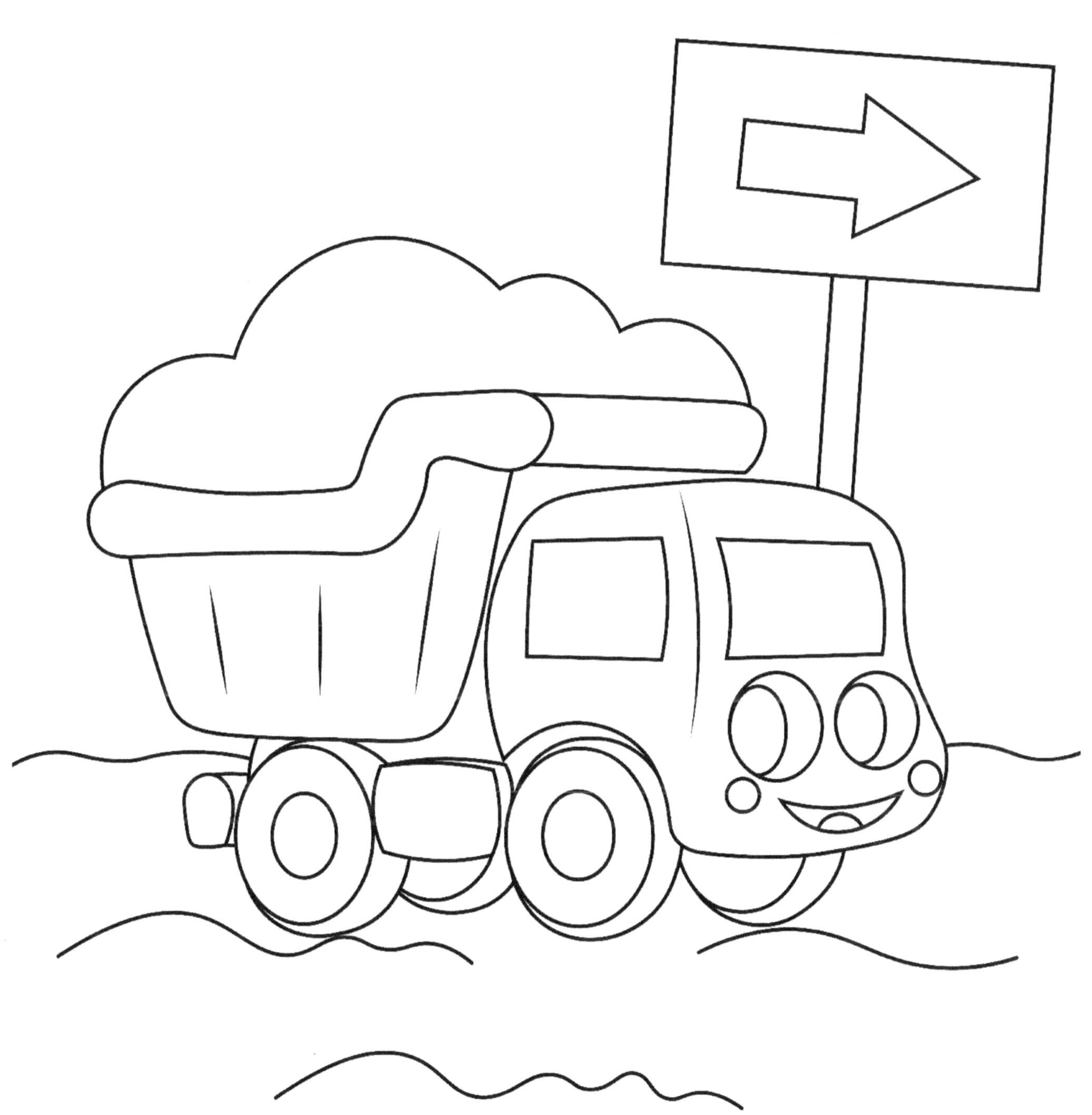